Leadership

with a

Twist of Yoga

Leadership

with a

Twist of Yoga

Shar McBee

SMB Publishing

LEADERSHIP WITH A TWIST OF YOGA
Copyright © 2018 by Shar McBee

For information contact :
www.JoyofLeadership.com

Editor Jose Mestre
Cover design by Luis Hurtado
ISBN: 978-0-9638560-8-1

First Edition: November 2018

Table of Contents

"Don't put a ceiling on yourself."

Oprah Winfrey

Welcome

My favorite model of a miserable manager is Charles Dickens' legendary character, Ebenezer Scrooge. He was "a squeezing, wrenching, grasping, scraping, clutching, covetous old sinner," according to Dickens. His most faithful employee, Bob Cratchit, obeyed him, yet feared him. Cratchit remained loyal to Scrooge for years and what did Scrooge do? He begrudged him one day off.

I'm drawn to the Scrooge story and his subsequent transformation because, unfortunately, I was a lot like him. As a young manager, I thought leadership was naturally adversarial. The boss is bossy and the employees are disgruntled. I was afraid of making a mistake which made me rigid. My fear of failing resulted in a lack of flexibility. I was intent on getting the job done but failed to note that I was creating poor relationships.

I didn't know it at the time, but with my lack of leadership skills, I was not alone. Every day millions of people report to work to a boss who never had one day of leadership training. Why are we surprised when new managers, who were never taught, don't know how to lead?

"Easy to attain, but difficult to maintain."

Yoga Master B.K.S. Iyengar

Welcome

I started out as a normal person with a normal job who wanted to be of service. At age 26, I began work on a voter registration drive in California. Participation exploded quickly. I suddenly found myself supervising over 500 people. The work was worthwhile but the people were challenging. It was hard. I spent many sleepless nights worrying and wondering, "Why is this so difficult?"

On one particularly bad day, I was exhausted. The situation had become too grim. I began to question my purpose in life. Could I make an impact? I had lost my will to continue, when a mentor saw my distress and intervened with this wonderful warning: "You've come a long way. Don't give up now."

She explained, "With so much coming at you, many people in your position would run away. Before you quit, consider this: How you embrace power, reveals everything. Are you strong enough to hold the power you are given?"

Then she smiled.

It was a turning point moment. A little advice at the right time helped me survive the stress. In the coming years, advice from wonderful mentors changed everything. Eventually, I learned that leadership is not getting people to do what I want them to do, but making it possible for them to succeed. With that understanding, it became one of life's most rewarding experiences. A career should not be about how to survive, but how to thrive on the harmony that arises when a group of people are working together at their highest potential. Because of the wise guidance I received, the time I spent in leadership positions was no longer painful; it was a pleasure.

As a motivational speaker, I've shared the advice you are about to read with over 150,000 people in live audiences and with millions more through the media. Encouraging people to accept leadership roles makes me happy. I love it when they recognize that *management doesn't have to mean misery*. If you are dedicated to doing a good job, whether you are an entrepreneur, work for a large corporation, volunteer for a nonprofit, or own your own business, if you supervise people this book is for you.

New managers tell me that they often feel isolated. Yet new managers rarely ask for help. Before they are promoted, many expect that advancement into management will result in accolades and a sense of accomplishment. Instead, they find themselves feeling tired and alone. Frustrated when people don't cooperate, they ditch their dreams. Discouraged when employees become a challenge, some quit the company they had previously loved. When they lose control and nobody is listening, many capable new managers morph into screaming meanies.

Stop! Don't do it. *Don't you dare become the big, bad boss like Scrooge.* It has been said that people are promoted to their level of incompetence. I don't believe it. *You are competent.* When you are feeling disrespected and harassed, don't give up. In spite of everything, you can be a successful manager. You just need assistance in dealing with the most valuable and important component of your new position – the people.

My goal is to inspire you to be the leader you want to be by offering you simple, concrete solutions to everyday challenges. How do you create cooperation? What makes people give you support? How do you turn reluctant employees into willing participants? This book addresses these issues and more perplexing, challenging, and illusive management mysteries.

As a leader, I hope you won't suffer like I did, or become pathetic like stingy old Scrooge. Instead, I'd like you to receive what you deserve – respect and admiration.

Welcome

How to use this book: Don't *believe* it. Try it. Test it for yourself. Before you begin, answer the question, "If you could get anything you want from this book, what do you want?" Be specific. Whatever your goals, make them crystal-clear and focus on your top priorities.

To be of service to the world, be of service in *your world*. Make a difference in the lives of those who work with you. Most of us have at least one former boss that we remember with gratitude; one who saw our potential and gave us a chance; recognized our talent and pointed it out; a boss who inspired our loyalty, trust and our excellence. Now that you are a manager, why shouldn't that great boss be you?

What is the twist of yoga? I began practicing yoga many years ago and it immediately made me feel calm, which was a surprise because at that time I thought yoga was about strength and athleticism. Later, I discovered that yoga is about unity, balance, and gratitude.

At the end of each chapter you will find a *Yoga Wisdom* section that will support you in applying the *Leadership with a Twist of Yoga* principles. Some of it is physical; some is a way of thinking about yourself and others. Science has proven over and over again how much the mind and body are connected. When we change our bodies (even just our breathing) it can change the way people relate to us.

In Sanskrit, yoga means union. Yoga can help you to renew and expand yourself through empowering others. In the *Yoga Wisdom* sections, you will learn about the true freedom that comes from detachment. As a leader, yoga can teach you to disengage from situations that might cause you to react emotionally. It will help curtail overconfidence which can cause you to make mistakes.

"Nature does not hurry, yet everything
is accomplished."

Lao Tzu

By keeping your ego and self-importance under control, the egos of others have nothing to compete against. Pride makes people hard. Desire makes them soft. Yoga makes them dynamic.

Yoga (unity) brings joy – the true joy that arises from within, not the false joy that comes from trying to force success. Chasing victories will never lead to happiness. To be happy and ultimately successful, we need to be willing to be led, and to be led, we need to learn how to surrender.

Yoga teaches surrender and stability. Picture a mountain. It is not intimidated by a storm. It surrenders to the circumstances and remains stable. Learning the yogic "Mountain Pose" and the philosophy behind it will help you avoid the pressure that comes with challenging situations. There's no need to act prematurely in a predicament, or jump to your first conclusion. When you learn to be still, standing steady and quiet like a mountain, you won't have to grasp for the quickest solution.

Yoga creates energy. Impatience scatters it. New endeavors always include chaos. The Mountain Pose helps you to relax during chaotic beginnings. When you learn the yogic concept of "stability before mobility," it will help you to be comfortable with non-action until the right thing to do becomes clear. This should provide greater opportunities, and make it possible to expand your horizons.

I used to be a regular expert guest on a television talk show. The producer advised me to, "Always know the answer. Never say you don't know." Later, when I had a big leadership position, pretending to know all the answers was perilous. Fortunately, yoga, which teaches patience and conservation of energy, gave me the self-confidence to admit, "I don't know."

True leadership is not being right, nor standing on top. It is supporting from the bottom and using diverse circumstances creatively. Also, a leadership position does not last forever; it is merely part of a cycle that one day will wane. Some day you, too, must surrender your power. Meanwhile, stay true to your convictions. Lead with integrity. Use your leadership opportunity to serve the higher good.

Chapter One: How to Create Cooperation

"Bah!" said Scrooge, "Humbug!"

Why settle for a STAR when you could go for a GALAXY?

You hire bright, strong individuals. You want them on your team. Then, what do you do when they express their strong individuality? One team member has a know-it-all attitude. Another one shows off an intellectual superiority. Yet another is a suck up. As their leader, how do you get a group of independent individuals to cooperate?

On a consulting job, my task was to rekindle a team that had once been led by the company's rising star. I was brought in because, after an initial success, the group fizzled. Months into a second project and mired in discord, the team couldn't get its new project off the ground.

At first glance, it was easy to see why management had high expectations for this team. Each individual was talented. The group leader was a strong, bright woman who stood out like a shining star. They all agreed that it was her expertise and hard work that had made the first project successful.

A star team with a star leader. You can understand why the new CEO had been wildly enthusiastic about them at first. But now he was worried.

The stars weren't shining so brightly. Although the CEO and the team members were proud of themselves for a job well done on the first project, at this point there was dissention. Enthusiasm was deteriorating. Morale was low. Several members of the team were actively looking for new jobs.

Because the CEO deferred so many decisions to the group leader, I interviewed her first. She was, as her teammates described her, brilliant. She was also opinionated and her opinions of the other team members were not pretty. She was convinced that if the job was going to get done, she had to do it herself. And she did. She surprised everyone with how much she could accomplish.

The team, however, didn't grow. It wasn't strong. The more responsibility she assumed, the less other people did. Although her individual work was shining, the group work was deteriorating. She was full of self-importance because of the early triumph, but now she was essentially working alone. Her backup team had fizzled and, as one person alone, she couldn't sustain the momentum. She knew that people were ready to quit but she didn't care.

The CEO desperately wanted to rebuild morale, so every person was interviewed and asked, "If you could do anything on the next project, what would you like to contribute?"

The CEO was stunned by their responses. People wanted to give a lot more than he suspected. Because they had appeared lackadaisical compared to his star employee, he thought they weren't interested in the second project. Actually, they were hurt that they weren't given more opportunities to share their unique talents and do what they knew best how to do.

Suddenly, a spark went off in the CEO's mind. All along, he had a galaxy of good people; a goldmine of talent; but he hadn't noticed because he was blinded by the light of one star employee.

Realizing this, everything changed. People were given responsibility. Each one got a piece of the pie. Participation exploded. Now those that had previously wanted to leave, stayed. Their new ideas were rich and pertinent to the project. No one had to be forced or coerced to work. In fact, when the second project was finally completed, the team couldn't wait to get going on a third assignment.

At last the CEO had an organization, rather than a group of disconnected individuals. He had esprit de corps among his workers. With a galaxy of good people, he no longer had to worry about what would happen if he lost his one star.

Individual work is weak. Teamwork is strong. New managers often make the mistake of depending on their star employees. Like this CEO, for an overwhelmed new manager, it is easy to rely heavily on them. Star employees love responsibility, but be careful. If you rely too much on one person, when he or she fizzles, you could become the falling star.

Should you stop a star from shining?

What do you do about a star? Stars stand out. They often have more connections, more experience, and more eagerness for getting the job done. They also disrupt discussions. They'll poison the atmosphere with an attitude of entitlement. Stars might act as if the ideas of their co-workers are nonsense. Don't believe it. If your stars bulldoze over the rest of the team, eventually they'll bulldoze over you, too.

"Harmony comes from joining together the disconnected."

Greek philosopher Heraclites
535-475 BC

Like the earth depends on the sun, you need your stars, and you need them to help build your team. One of the best ways to turn individual stars into team players is to turn them into mentors for others. That's what happened to the woman in this story. The CEO put her in charge of the mentoring program where she became a star at developing future team leaders.

If you are a manager, you have probably been the star yourself. You've probably worked for a star, too. In my career I have reported to a star and I have been the star. I know how it feels to get all the glory. I also know how it feels to have my talent unused and my ideas unwanted. Frankly, I don't like either situation. My favorite, most successful projects have been the ones where the whole group shines.

Imagine this: Two hospitals. Two emergency rooms. A medical doctor works at both, dividing his time between the two. At one, the work is extremely demanding. The doctor is given a huge case load and very little rest. At the other emergency room, the work is less arduous. The pay is the same at both. Yet, in selecting shifts, the doctor chooses the hospital where the work is the most strenuous.

What would make a doctor choose a hospital where he has to work harder?

A hospital emergency room is a perpetual motion machine. On the first day that it opens for business, an emergency room unlocks its doors and never shuts them again. It is open twenty-four hours a day, seven days a week, fifty-two weeks a year. The workday has no beginning and no end because all day, every day, there is a constant rollover of staff and patients.

The doctor that I'm talking about works at two emergency rooms in a large city. He says, "People do this kind of work because they want to be of service to humanity, but the pressure can be overwhelming."

Why on earth would an experienced professional like this physician choose the hospital with the *most pressure*? The one that is the most demanding?

The doctor says, "We have an administrator who is a kindred spirit and a genius. She's a former nurse who sees her job as primarily to give respect and empathy for the difficulties that others face. Her service is to make it possible for others to serve. She cares for those who care."

Instead of focusing on getting her staff to do what she needs done, this remarkable manager focuses on giving them her support. She runs the ER like it is a living organism. She nourishes everyone who works there. When people arrive at work, they are recognized and acknowledged. No one goes unnoticed. All are kept in the loop. Her point of view is that her staff is outstanding, therefore she receives outstanding results.

The doctor says, "Her attitude is really contagious. Abuse of sick leave does not exist there. The work at the other hospital is less demanding, but when I'm selecting shifts, I have a definite preference for the hospital where this nurse has created a work culture that is so exceptional."

What is this manager's secret? Why would professional people choose to work with her, even though the job is easier somewhere else?

Connection is key. Daily she communicates with everyone so they all feel connected to her and to each other. This manager is willing to receive the opinions of her staff with an open mind. This is greatly appreciated, so her staff gives back. They are loyal, dependable and helpful to her. They feel connected to her so they give her their best.

Understanding and shared bonds is another reason for this manager's success. As a former nurse, she knows the pressure that the medical personnel endure. Many managers make decisions without understanding what those decisions actually mean to the staff. True understanding is not intellectual. It's warm and it's personal.

A big part of yoga is service to others. This administrator knows that and she created an atmosphere where they would want to serve, even in a difficult work environment. Policies cannot cover every contingency. Sometimes a policy can be absurd or even dangerous. A know-it-all attitude will prevent a manager from knowing the staff's real needs.

The big, bad boss resorts to manipulating and intimidating people. When you are connected to your co-workers, you don't have to coerce them. The nurse/manager at the emergency room has created a situation where she can actually influence her staff when she needs to. People follow, assist, and rally around those with whom they feel a connection.

Scrooge was "Secret, and self-contained and solitary as an oyster."

Leadership with a Twist of Yoga
principle to remember:

To Lead is to Connect

Do you lead from the front? Or from the middle?

Why do managers erect barriers and distance themselves from the people they lead?

Decisions made by a group, on average, are better than decisions made by individuals, according to a study conducted by Gayle W. Hill at Michigan State University. The study found that by pooling and aggregating disparate pieces of information, groups form better decisions.

Most managers feel pressured to make good decisions, yet many are reluctant to seek advice from the people they lead. On a consulting job, I had a new manager tell me *NOT* to ask the opinions of her team. Everyone else on the team had worked there for years. She was brand new, but she didn't want to know their thoughts. What on earth was she thinking?

The following is an odd illustration, but you might find it helpful. Try to remember the first time you baked cookies. (If you've never baked cookies, imagine it.)

I whipped up my first batch as a young bride during a time I call the Granola Days. We were trying to be healthy, so I bought the most nutritious cookie ingredients I could find: brown sugar, whole wheat flour, oats, nuts, and raisins.

My husband and some of his tennis buddies were bantering jokes around in the living room while I was in the kitchen mixing up the cookie dough.

I stirred the ingredients together, put small dollops on the tray, and placed it in the oven. In next to no time the house filled with the fragrance of cookies baking. The anticipation built. The guys were salivating. Ten minutes later I pulled the tray from the oven. To my great dismay, there were no cookies. The tray was full of soup.

"What happened?" asked my distressed husband.

"I forgot to mix in the flour," I replied, forlorned.

Without the flour, there were no cookies. The flour is what connects all the other elements. My great ingredients were worthless because I left out the one essential component that would connect them together.

New managers often strive for prominence. They struggle to maintain a position out in front of the team, which is why the one mentioned above didn't want to ask the people who reported to her for their advice. She wanted to appear strong and competent, but actually she was insecure.

I used to think that the way to be outstanding was to stand out. I thought the role of a leader was to shine like a bright red cherry on the top of a cake. This took a lot of effort and, at best, the results were temporary. Through painful experiences and sleepless nights, I learned that truly outstanding leaders don't try to stand out. They are not like the cherry. They are more like the flour. The flour is the most humble ingredient. At the same time, it is the most essential. In fact, you may not even notice it unless it is missing.

This is key to the *Leadership with a Twist of Yoga* method: Succeed like nature. Nature's work is invisible, behind the scenes, yet nothing is more creative or more abundant. You don't even notice it until, suddenly, the blossom blooms, the sky turns purple, or the tree is covered with fruit.

You, too, can create spectacular results if you learn to lead like nature, behind the scenes. This doesn't mean you never stand in front; it means you don't lead with your ego. Instead of striving to stand out, you become a connector. You make sure that others feel included which will help *them* succeed.

When people feel included, they'll support you. If they feel excluded, they'll undermine you. People feel happiest when they feel they belong. So, if you want people to cooperate with you and with each other, be like the flour – become the connector.

When you create a connection between people, it builds morale. If your staff members are feeling left out or they are not communicating; if there is opposition or estrangement, they will not make good decisions or perform vital assignments together.

Scott Edwards, Senior Vice President of On Air Promotions & Operations at Fox Broadcasting, created the WITTy method for his new managers to implement. He says, "Of course, it stands for *We're In This Together*. And that philosophy can be very compelling and unifying in any creative, scientific, logistical, social, sales-oriented, manufacturing, agricultural, medicinal, or otherwise corporate environment. But it's not just a saying, it has to be a way of being; it has to be something embodied behaviorally. If I give a suggestion that turns out not to work, I take ownership. And if I give one that receives high praise and endorsement, I make sure to share the credit."

Scott continues, "At Fox Broadcasting, in the On-Air Promo Department, this is one of our guiding sentiments. And it lives and breathes in another saying we have, which is whatever we do, we do it together. Does this mean that every employee embraces these and enacts them 100% of the time? Not a chance. Because we're dealing with fallible humans, who bring their issues with them. They show up daily with their baggage, their unique level of professional training (or lack thereof), their conditioned reactions, their routine thinking, their traditional models of problem solving, etc. But, as a leader of people, and manager of resources, at the very least you can present an idea and inform the team they are expected to rise to the occasion by embracing and living the idea daily. When an employee doesn't, you deal with it."

Joanne Vaughn's husband served in the Foreign Service for twenty-seven years during which time the Vaughn family lived all over the world. Joanne says, "When you ask people where they were the happiest, you learn what builds community. People could be unhappy – even in comfortable assignments like Paris. On the other hand, people could be happy in challenging assignments like West Africa or North Sumatra."

She says, "When we asked Foreign Service families about their favorite posting, it was never the comfortable locations. Invariably it was the hardest with the least comforts."

It seems strange. Why would families fondly remember the years they lived without supermarkets or cars; when they had only sporadic electricity, no washing machines or even refrigeration? Joanne says, "They had to bond to survive. When people help each other, know each other, they work better with each other."

According to Joanne Vaughn, "Friendship trumps a lot of difficulties." When people bond, they are willing to overlook impediments. When they don't, even a talented team won't perform up to snuff.

I received an email from a PhD at the National Institute of Health. She has a job that should be exciting for a scientist, but she said, "My boss is too busy with other things and a lot of 'death by neglect' is happening. We are talented scientists, but we are ignored."

Connection (like baking) is an organic process. You can't rush it. Be patient. Cooperation will grow as the connections develop, so allow it to take its proper course. Real influence can only be gradual. Trying to force connections between you and your team is unwise. If you push them, people may misjudge your good intentions. Take time to create your connections, and then people will have time to see that you are sincere, making them more likely to cooperate with you.

US and THEM

Picture this: You are in a large auditorium. At opposite ends of the room there are two posters hanging from the ceiling. One poster says US and the other says THEM. Now, I'd like you to choose one of the posters and stand under it.

Will you choose to stand under a poster labeled US or a poster labeled THEM?

I have posed this question to over 100,000 audience members. 99% choose US. It's an amazing percentage. There are few questions that elicit this kind of consensus. As a leader, can you see why this information is important to you?

Human beings want to feel included. In fact, to belong is a basic human need. When people feel involved, they'll be there for you. When they feel ignored or left out, they won't.

If your staff feels connected to you and to each other:

- How would that improve your productivity?
- Could it perk up your customer service?
- In what ways would it boost employee retention?

Bottom line: *It will cut costs.* We are not talking about "soft skills" or "feel good" management. Your financial success depends on how well you make others feel included.

Cathy Sterling was in a New York audience when I asked people to choose between US and THEM. At the time, she was facing a dilemma. The membership at her homeowners' association was dwindling. She and her neighbors depend on the dues to maintain the community's common space and keep it in a quality condition.

Cathy didn't know how to turn the bad situation around. She had worked hard to create social events that people would want to attend, but membership continued to decline. In a few years the situation would be even worse because the association was not attracting young families.

After hearing about *US* and *THEM*, Cathy realized that the problem was *Old-timers* vs. *Newcomers*. Long-time members had created an insider atmosphere that was not welcoming. New people weren't joining because they didn't feel included.

How do you cope with Old-timers vs. Newcomers?

This is what Cathy did: She invited all the property owners (members and non-members) to a reception. She asked the members to go out of their way to welcome new faces. She announced to the non-members, "When you leave here today, whether you join or not, we want you to feel that you are one of us. We want you to know that you are wanted."

Excited, Cathy exclaims, "People joined! Previously, there were factions; now everyone feels they belong. Before, almost all of our members were retired people. We now have young couples with children." In two years, the Mohican Lake Taxpayers Civic Association went from 52 members to 124 members. A 238% increase!

To be inclusive requires a decision (a firm decision) because the pull to let the *US* and *THEM* situation remain as it is can be strong. Some leaders feel that it does no harm. Some don't even notice. Leaders are insiders themselves so they don't recognize it when others are left out. It isn't painful to them, so they think that people don't care. This is delusion.

All organizations have insiders and outsiders, long-term employees and new hires, familiar customers and those who stumble in your door. It doesn't take any more time, (but it does take more effort) to reach out to people you don't know. Both you and your staff must make the effort.

I took my dog Ben, a Lhasa Apso, to a new veterinarian. We arrived early for the 10 am appointment. When I stopped at the reception desk the receptionist was talking on the telephone, so I took a seat. At 10:30 am we were still waiting. Although there were now two "receptionists," neither said one word to us. They talked on the telephone and to each other.

I don't think Ben noticed but I was annoyed. Finally, I stood up and said, "It's been a half hour and no one has acknowledged that we are here. I don't want a vet who is so unwelcoming." Ben and I left. When I got home, there was a voicemail message from the veterinarian.

"This is Dr. …. I've spent a fortune on training my staff, sending them to seminars. They still don't know how to treat my clients. I'm sorry it happened to you, but your comments today showed them what happens when people are ignored. Thank you for saying what you did."

Are you surprised? There's more.

It was a small waiting room. Ben and I were alone. While we waited, the veterinarian walked into the reception area twice. He looked through a filing cabinet and spoke to a person on the telephone. He didn't' speak to us. He didn't even look at us.

Later, his voicemail message said that he had spent a fortune on training his staff. Why, I wondered, didn't he train himself, too? The vet had let *US and THEM* develop into *BOSS vs. STAFF*. In some languages, the word "devil" means *to divide*.

"The biggest disease today is the feeling of being unwanted."

Mother Teresa

Why in the devil did he think a *BOSS* vs. *STAFF* attitude could fix *US* and *THEM?* All it did was divide him from his team.

In *BOSS* vs. *STAFF* circumstances, when an obstinate boss thinks he's good and the employees are bad, it causes first-rate employees to leave. Morale is miserable. Creativity is crushed. The boss winds up surrounded by yes-people because the people of quality are gone.

Then, the yes-people create *US* and *THEM* among the other employees. They may have been polite when you hired them, but once they consider themselves to be part of the in-crowd, they take on an air of superiority, behaving as if they are a cut above the rest.

US and *THEM* can lead to people being ostracized or criticized. It's *US* and *THEM* when one or two people dominate the discussion while others sit mute. If people are using body language and rolling their eyes to express displeasure, it is a sure sign that the divisive old devil, *US* and *THEM* has crawled into your midst.

The human cost of *US* and *THEM* is huge. Eliminate *US* and *THEM* and you'll put the joy into leadership. Unlike the veterinarian, you'll keep your customers. Like the homeowners' association, your business will grow. Because your entire staff feels included in your inner circle, they'll cooperate with you.

Two years later, the same veterinarian was in the audience when I spoke at a Chamber of Commerce Leadership Day. He approached me and said, "I'm embarrassed to admit this because it took me awhile, but I finally realized what happened. The problem wasn't my employees, was it?" He assured me that he has become more welcoming.

WHO or *HOW*

When you are the leader, you have probably noticed that people are eager to give you advice. My advice is this: Let them. Then, your challenge becomes what do you do with their recommendations? Can you accept suggestions without growing overwhelmed?

One day I received a call from a businessman who was involved in quite a few philanthropies. He had read my first book, *To Lead is to Serve,* and liked the philosophy. He wanted to help spread the word. In a generous way, he started giving me marketing advice.

I was interested. However, as he offered more and more suggestions, I began to feel fatigued. Holding the telephone with one hand and propping my head up with the other, I struggled to listen as I slowly sank lower and lower into a chair. It felt like I was drowning.

With each new idea the businessman suggested, I wondered, "How will I do that? How will I find the time? How will I find the resources?" I dutifully took pages of notes and when we finally hung up, I felt mired in a monumental "to do" list. Although I hadn't done one thing, I was exhausted.

I knew it was a good opportunity. Unless I acted on his suggestions quickly, his enthusiasm would go away. I'd lose him if I didn't follow through. But it felt hard.

How do you let people participate without becoming overwhelmed by their advice?

Soon after the call from the businessman, the telephone rang again. It was the president of the board of directors of an organization that had recruited me to chair a fundraising dinner. In the process, I had observed some challenging dynamics between people and the inner workings of the organization. It seemed to me that a few small changes would make a big difference and I was waiting for the right moment to share my ideas with the president.

"Oh, good," I thought, "here's my chance." I launched into offering my advice, but before I had finished, she interrupted.

"This is too much," she said, "I feel overwhelmed."

My intention was not to deluge her with ideas and information. I didn't want to create a giant "to do" list for her. I wanted to relieve some of her burden, not add to it. So, I stopped.

Later, I thought about the two conversations. The businessman had the best intentions. His advice came from the place of a big heart, yet he inundated me with information. My intentions were also lofty, yet I overwhelmed the person I was offering advice to.

Why does this happen? Why is it hard to take other people's suggestions? And even harder to act on them?

Two weeks later, someone came to my office with an explanation. Deborah DeWitt is a master chef who owned a successful catering company in Austin, Texas. I told her what happened and she said, "If you want your business to grow, don't stop people from giving you their suggestions."

"But advice can be intense," I objected. "It's overwhelming to be bombarded with propositions."

"You have to let everyone give their advice," Deborah said, "and when you hear their ideas, don't ask *how*."

I still didn't understand.

"Logic will get you from A to B.
Imagination will take you everywhere."

Einstein

Deborah explained, "Don't ask *how*. '*How* will I do that? *How* will I find the resources? *How* will I recruit the people? *How* will I raise the money?' When you ask *how*, you might overwhelm yourself."

"Instead, ask *who*," she said. "*Who* likes to do that? *Who* knows about it? *Who's* interested? *Who* could finance it? This allows the conversation to continue. When you stop the flow of ideas, you block people from helping you."

A light bulb went on. It was exactly what happened when the businessman offered his advice to me. I asked myself, "*How* am I going to do all of this?" which blocked the flow. In the case of the board chair, it was the same situation.

If the president of the board of directors had allowed me to share my ideas with her, I would have become more involved in her organization. If I had allowed the businessman to share his ideas with me, he could have helped me with my business. In both cases, asking *how* resulted in a feeling of overwhelm. It cut off the opportunity to cooperate. By asking *who*, the relationships could have continued.

Yoga is about balance and stability. Being caught up in the *HOW* can cause distress and knock us off balance. When our thoughts and feelings about ourselves are stable, we are open to input from the outside. We are open to discovering the *WHO*.

The *WHO* or *HOW* method is a way to grow without growing overwhelmed. A good idea doesn't mean that *you* have to implement it. Thinking you have to do everything yourself is a challenge in leadership. In yoga this is called doership. When you weigh yourself down with too many tasks and fill your mind with a magnitude of concerns, other people can't help you. Busyness is an impenetrable wall. Thinking that only you know how things should be done will result in "only you" doing the work.

The burden of having everything on your shoulders is heavy. When you become the doer, you block people from giving you a hand. It prevents you from connecting with others and prevents them from cooperating with you.

Have you heard (or said) words like these?

- We tried that. It won't work.
- We don't do it that way. We've always done it this way.

These are *HOW* words. "This is how we do it." *HOW* words stop people from helping you. They put up a barricade and disconnect you from people who want to be of assistance. Durability requires flexibility. People will quickly give up on you when you act as if you know everything.

Asking *WHO* is inclusive. It can help you to lighten up. Use the word *WHO* and see what happens. *WHO* has done that? *WHO* likes to? *WHO* knows about it?

Fortunately, the businessman didn't give up on me. His name is Garrick Colwell and two years after that initial conversation we teamed up and presented seminars together.

BESTOW to GROW

Scrooge viewed them with a detestation and disgust.

There is something that will make a huge impact on the success you receive. It will not cost you time. It will not cost you money. It's something you must give. However, when you give it, you don't give it away. Giving it leaves you with more.

Do you know what it is?

Enormous strife had developed between the two founding partners of a technology company. They had launched the business together and now one partner wanted to sell because he decided the other partner didn't respect him.

It was almost like a divorce. He became so stuck about the disrespect, he couldn't do business with the other any longer. Their common goal had disappeared.

An arbitrator called the two partners together and asked one, "Why do you care if he respects you?"

The partner replied, "He doesn't show up at my presentations. I'm sales. He's technical. Without him, it's hard to close the sales."

There was silence in the room.

Finally, the other partner spoke: "I don't respect him because he doesn't close the sales."

Disrespect is immediately perceived by other people. When we decide that someone is hopeless, we make it hard for him to change. Uncertainty paralyzes people. When people feel respected, they feel safe. Feeling disrespected drains away their courage. They don't work at optimum. They are not likely to speak up when problems arise. They'll let things go, often until it's too late. The two partners had once worked well together. Now they despised each other.

When we give our respect, it is usually reciprocal. It leads to mutual appreciation. It allows both sides to suspend judgment and keep an open mind about the other. People do their best work when they feel respected. It makes them feel free to offer suggestions. Respect can be more important than money as a motivator. It can be more important than a title. In his short novel *The Old Man and the Sea*, Ernest Hemingway said respect is more important than life.

"Have the courage to follow your heart and intuition."

Steve Jobs

Between the two partners, one wanted respect even though he wasn't closing the sales; the other wanted sales but he wasn't giving his respect. What they didn't realize is that to succeed both required the other.

BESTOW respect and your success will GROW

Respected and *connected* are like *getting* and *giving.* They are one. Respect is something we must bestow, or the team won't grow. Of course, sometimes unity is impossible and we have to let people go. But usually, you'll find that when you cultivate a team that feels respected, they'll also feel connected. When there is no connection, your team is likely to become paralyzed and will disintegrate under pressure.

Gerhardt – The fairest of them all?

Everyone wanted Gerhardt to go. Not long before, people were clamoring to be close to him. Gerhardt used to be on top of the world. He was charismatic. His reputation was widespread. At the same time, he was cocky, bored by routine, and strutted around like he was God's gift to humanity.

With his medical education and commanding physique, Gerhardt appeared perfect for the part when the Board of Directors selected him as the Executive Director of a non-profit that provided health care to needy children. When Gerhardt arrived, the organization had volunteers and employees who were highly educated and generous people.

Gerhardt won the appointment over several long-term staff members, accomplished people who had built the organization, written grants, and developed donations. He walked into a well-oiled machine…and sucked it dry.

At first, he concentrated on ingratiating himself to the large donors and people of influence. Back at the office, he was crushing his employees. Monique had been in charge during the interim. As head of human resources, she had hired most of the staff and worked well with them.

Despite his credentials, Gerhardt had no leadership experience. He sensed Monique's lack of confidence in him, which compounded his anxieties. He didn't trust her, but he kept pushing more work on her while hovering around, expecting the worst. This made her feel demeaned. It undermined her abilities. One day he lost his temper and told Monique that she was a cancer on the organization. Monique quit.

Now, most of the staff wished he would quit. Still, Gerhardt remained proud and unaware that he was dragging the organization down because he stayed isolated behind a wall of sycophants. He was hypersensitive to criticism. Even helpful suggestions he took as slights. He turned against those that complained. He retaliated and was punitive. He never listened. He pretended to, sometimes even said that he agreed, and then did exactly as he pleased, persisting in futile efforts. Eventually he alienated the largest donor.

Finally, the Board woke up to the cost of hiring a man with a doctor's title but who had no people skills. When Gerhardt lost his job, not one person tried to defend him.

Treating people with respect is a way of protecting your own future. Being the big, bad boss hurts when you fall. It also hurts when you are falling. And, if truth be told, being a bad boss even hurts when you are on top because everyone can see how badly you are behaving.

You might know a Gerhardt. His superiors found him utterly charming, but in his own office, he was a petty tyrant. People were so intimidated, they couldn't think clearly when they met with him. Bosses like Gerhardt leave behind a trail of resentful relationships and more mini-tyrants, because people emulate what the person at the top does.

He became uppity when he was asked to resign, saying, "I have the best education in this place." He was told, "It doesn't matter how many degrees you have. You don't know how to motivate, inspire, and energize your team. You are not a leader."

It took Gerhardt over a year to find another job. His new position was far less prestigious. Hopefully he changed, and the people who work with him today are reaping the benefits of what Gerhardt learned from his fall.

What can we learn from Gerhardt? Most people become humble and respectful when they are down. The challenge is to do it when you are up. Respect trumps title. Arrogance made him indifferent to suffering. His defensive attitude prevented him from learning from his mistakes. By exalting some and disparaging others, Gerhardt created a chasm instead of a connection. From a yogic point of view, he cut off the energy of his co-workers.

Believe it or not, your job as the leader is not to get other people to do the work. Your job is to make it possible for them to succeed. This is often the hardest thing for new managers to grasp. After all, you were promoted because you know how to do a good job. If you say, "For this to be done right, I'm going to have to do it myself," you'll wind up burnt out, tired, and as remorseful as Gerhardt. In the long run, the best way to get the job done right is to build a tight team to do it.

Unity is vital for human beings. Build your connections today and people will be there for you in the future.

"Alone we can do so little; together we can do so much."

Helen Keller

Yoga Wisdom

Stability Before Mobility

In Sanskrit, the word "yoga" means "union." Yoga is not about *THEM*. It is about *US* as the homeowners' association and the veterinarian's office stories demonstrate. In the West we've come to think of yoga as just the physical postures. Exercise. But it is much more than that. Yoga unites your mind, your body and your emotions. Forward bends are relaxing and calm your nerves. Backbends are invigorating. Twists increase flexibility and make you more open-minded. Wouldn't that be helpful to you in a leadership position?

I've been writing and speaking about leadership for years and practicing yoga even longer. I first recognized the connection between leadership and yoga while I was helping a corporate executive prepare a speech. His demeanor was weak. He didn't have oomph. It was disappointing, so I asked him to stand in the warrior pose to practice the speech.

He got better. Hmmmm. But it still wasn't strong enough. Finally, I said, "God gave you that big body. Use it to serve." Wow. Something happened to him. He looked like a Picasso painting going into alignment. He stood up straight, shoulders back, relaxed. No longer slouching. No longer limp. Both he and the speech became powerful. He went home pleased, as was I.

Warrior Pose

Virabhadrasana II

The next day his wife called me and asked, "What did you do to him?"

"I don't know," I replied, "What do you mean?"

"He came home transformed," she explained, and then continued, "He has always been afraid that other people are frightened of big, black men. His entire life he has tried to make himself look smaller. When you said, 'God gave you that big body. Use it to serve,' he suddenly saw himself in a new light."

He had to be stable in his own body to be effective. He had to know who he was before he could reach out. A balanced attitude makes it possible to influence others in a positive way.

Bradley Horowitz, VP Product at Google, says "The tech world is a highly unstructured environment. You wake up and the world has changed. Whether through new competition or a new government regulation, your job can change on a dime. You constantly must make plans in the wake of an ever-changing world. If you can stay balanced through it, embrace the paradox, not be reactive, and still have goals but be adaptable, you'll be able to stay above the fray and maintain your integrity."

Staying balanced helps you keep your mind open about possibilities and free yourself of the idea that a thing can't work. Unlikely things happen every day. Bradley says, "A career is a journey. The higher you rise, or the higher the company rises, the more drama is associated with your role. Almost daily, the world presents ever more epic challenges that find their way to you. It becomes especially important to dampen the drama and come from a position of balance to get through it."

"Yoga and leadership are not very different," he says, "They both teach us to think deeper than the fluctuations of the mind and get in touch with our core. From that balanced place we can make good decisions."

To become a warrior at work, maybe what you need is a warrior pose. "Stability before mobility" will help you in a yoga posture and in your life. The warrior pose creates courage; increases focus; improves your balance; it opens the heart; it works on your shoulders, your neck, your legs and your back. Do you think that would be good for you as a leader?

In a leadership role, you are a natural conduit providing nourishment for the people you lead. Your own nourishment is at issue, too. What you feed yourself includes not only food, but also the thoughts you think. Just as you need wholesome food, you also need to be careful about what enters your mind. If your thoughts are balanced, you will naturally have a good effect on others. When you allow stress to enter your mind, the people around you suffer.

Seema Eckler, Strategy & Operations Consultant at Deloitte Consulting, travels from city to city, constantly on the road almost every week. She is newly married and just bought her first home. She says, "Life is moving a million miles an hour. Yoga helps me with my stress. It helps me slow down for a little bit. My yoga practice is my link to feeling centered and grounded."

Yoga has been a lifelong practice for Seema. Sometimes less, sometimes more. But she always comes back to it because it makes her feel centered and she feels accomplished afterwards.

According to Seema, yoga principles also relate to working with people. She says, "At work, a good team needs a positive environment. Each person focusing on self-improvement is important. Yoga is a community of positive and supportive people that brings me energy. When you are practicing the poses, you only compare yourself to you and where you are. It is not about comparing yourself to how the people around you are doing the pose. At work, when you don't feel that everyone is competitive, you can speak up safely."

Seema's father told her that a career is a marathon, not a sprint. She says, "Yoga teaches me to slow down, breathe, and work through the poses. At work, I try to slow down and remember it's not a sprint."

She says, "The company culture at Deloitte is they invest in people, wanting them to be happy. The company cares about people, and I do, too. I consult in procurement technologies. If a company wants to buy office supplies, for instance, or professional services, I help them implement a system that enables a more efficient purchasing process. Yoga makes you more efficient because when you are not stressed out, it removes clutter in the mind and prevents brain fog."

What is yoga? If you are an advanced hatha yoga student, you may find this simplistic, but as Einstein said, "If the solution is simple, God is answering."

Yoga is not a twisted body. Not someone lying on a bed of nails. Not a technique nor an exercise. Yoga is about being in balance....stilling the fluctuations of the mind, according to the ancient definition in Patanjali's Yoga Sutras.

As a leader, you need balance so you no longer reel between hope and fear, expansion and contraction, pain and pleasure, success and failure. When you are in balance you function at your best. Your natural abilities flow out. You have more energy and experience more happiness and contentment. Would Gerhardt's experience have unfolded differently if he had known this?

Remember: the word yoga means "union" in Sanskrit. When your body, mind, emotions and energy are in alignment, you'll do the best work and be the best that you can be as a leader. When you are out of balance, you are a big mess. Tom, the man who was preparing the speech was tangled in a basic human struggle

"To thine own self be true."

Shakespeare

between contraction and expansion. Contraction to protect himself and the basic human desire to expand, to grow, to do all that he can do.

Yoga teaches that trying to avoid pain and seek pleasure gets you nowhere. With stability, you lighten up. You can laugh and enjoy the pleasure of playing the role of the person in charge. Lighthearted leaders are fondly remembered.

There are eight limbs of yoga. The physical postures (asanas) are only one limb called "hatha yoga." *Ha* means sun. *Tha* means moon. Through hatha yoga you root yourself to the earth which makes you stable enough to reach for the stars.

The *Leadership with a Twist of Yoga* method is a journey. It can be taken by anyone. Through unity (yoga) we tear down walls that stand between us and the people we work with. Tom had built a wall to protect himself and it walled him in, kept him down. It limited his ability to be his best.

This is an endless cycle with we human beings. We have a problem; find a solution; then the solution becomes a new problem. His problem was fear of being feared for his big body. The solution was to crouch and make himself look smaller. But the "solution" became a problem when he wanted to expand.

Yoga is about uniting all parts of ourselves. He couldn't be successful until he was stable with who he actually was. He went on to become the CEO of a huge international organization.

True yoga is not exercise. It is a way of developing balance, becoming firm, calm, and confident. It concerns resolving inner conflicts and being at peace with yourself which makes it possible for you to understand others. *Leadership with a Twist of Yoga* is about fulfilling your destiny.

Be who you are. Start where you are. NOW. Exactly as you are. Whether you are beginning a new yoga practice or a new leadership role, start with one step. Lao Tzu said, "The journey of a thousand miles begins with a single step." Yoga teaches us to focus on each step. If you are all over the map, you are just as lost as someone without a map. If you only focus on the goal, you'll miss a lot of magical moments.

When you feel safe and content, you want to expand. When you feel afraid, you want to contract. Yoga doesn't deny either. Both are part of the natural flow of life. As a leader you need to employ all aspects of yourself to take you to your destination.

Do you know what keeps a river flowing forward? The banks. The earth on the banks contain and sustain the river to move boldly onward. Without both river banks the water will flow out sideways and lose its momentum. Again, a move toward balance is a move toward a much stronger position.

I used to be a journalist covering the music industry. Often, when a new recording was about to be released the company would hold a listening party. If everyone in attendance liked it, they would *not* release it. Does this surprise you? It surprised me. I thought it was weird (to not release a record that everyone liked.) They only released it when most people liked it, but some hated it. After I learned through yoga that balance is necessary to keep things moving forward, then I understood. Like the river banks, both sides (both points of view) make a contribution.

For you to succeed as an effective leader, create strong connections to keep your career moving forward, and remember this principle: stability before mobility.

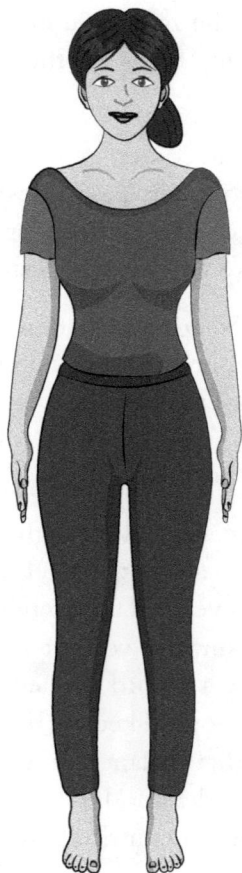

Mountain Pose

Tadasana

Tadasana – The Mountain Pose

Important: Before you begin practicing, PLEASE find an experienced teacher. Or, at least, a good book about the physical practice of yoga. Not all yoga poses are suitable for everyone. It is possible to injure yourself so listen to instructions and listen to your own body. Be careful.

Before you advance to the warrior pose, start with Tadasana, the mountain pose which is something you can do at work. Tadasana increases strength, power and mobility. It gives you confidence and courage. Improves posture. Firms the abdomen and buttocks. Relieves sciatica. Reduces flat feet.

- Stand with your feet together. If possible, stand with the bases of your big toes touching.
- Lift and spread your toes as you balance your weight on both feet.
- Lift the knee caps and firm your thigh muscles, turning the tops of the thighs slightly inward.
- Reach the top of your head toward the sky. Keep your chin parallel to the floor.
- Relax your arms, extended at your sides. Roll the shoulders back and down, keeping the sternum chest lifted.
- Widen your shoulder blades and press them forward. Release the trapezius down. This action alone will help you develop the muscles necessary to avoid looking like someone who is constantly hunching over a computer.
- Hold for about 30 seconds.

Gems to Remember

Go for a Galaxy

Star Employee vs. the Team

To Lead is to Connect

Emergency Room Manager

Do you Lead from the Middle?

The Cookies & the WITTy method

Us and Them

Newcomers vs. Old-timers

Who or How

Do You Let People Give You Advice?

Bestow to Grow

(dis)Respectful Partners

Tadasana – The Mountain Pose

Confidence, Courage and Balance

Exercise for Success

1. The CEO with the star employee: What happened to make the CEO recognize his galaxy of good people? How will you apply it to your work?
2. The emergency room nurse/manager: How did she earn the loyalty of the doctor? What could you learn from her?
3. The homeowners' association: How did the organization increase membership? Can you apply this to your organization, perhaps for customers? What will you do?
4. The businessman giving his guidance: What makes it possible to take advice? How will you employ this?
5. The two tech partners: What was missing? How did they save their partnership? What can you take away and use from their story?
6. In what ways will you apply "To Lead is to Connect"?

"Courage is what it takes to stand up and speak. Courage is also what it takes to sit down and listen."

Sir Winston Churchill

Chapter Two: How to Motivate People to Listen to You

Scrooge walked out with a growl.

A coworker and I were driving through the countryside on the way to a seminar. As usual, she was talking about herself. I listened as she chattered nonstop for fifty minutes. Eventually she paused and asked, "What have you been up to?"

"I'm writing a new book," I replied.

"Oh," she interrupted, "I was thinking of writing a book." Then she talked about her book idea for another thirty minutes.

Some people just talk too much. Why? Some are afraid of not being understood. Some think out loud. Some are insecure and want to impress you. Whatever the reason, these people are unaware of how they affect others. Do you know the feeling when you're trying to end a conversation and they don't notice? When you are backing away and they keep talking?

I'm happy to say that this chapter will help you with these people. You probably won't turn them into listeners, but you will be heard and you will know how to use listening to become a better leader.

You expect people to listen to you. You want them to listen. You need them to listen. But do they listen to you?

Steve, a Texas businessman, owns a design agency. One day he called my office. He had been in the audience three weeks earlier when I spoke to a group of business owners in Austin, Texas. On the phone he said, "Me and my dad bought a ranch up in the hills. To get to our land we need a right of way across our neighbor's land. For three years he has refused to give us the right of way."

Steve explained how they had begged and cajoled the neighbor, reasoned with him, justified and rationalized their point of view. They pointed out to the neighbor how much they needed to get to their land. All they wanted was for the neighbor to be reasonable. At first, they hoped he would be. But no. Years had gone by. They had spent hours talking to him and still had no right of way.

What should they do? What would you do?

In the past, in situations when I really wanted to be heard, I used to believe that I should speak first. I would arrive at a meeting thinking, "I have to speak right away because this is important." If someone else was droning on, I would become impatient. In fact, I wouldn't hear a word of what was being said because I was so anxious to speak. I was certain that my information was essential to the group and they would agree if I could just get them to listen to me. I discovered that speaking first did not make an impact. It didn't work.

Getting people to listen is a challenge. Getting them to hear you is a greater challenge. Most people are more interested in what they have to say than in what you want to tell them.

When I had hundreds of people reporting to me, I didn't have time to cajole them into listening. But I needed them to listen. I tried dozens of approaches. I read the advice of professionals and chased clues like a detective tracking down a lead. Nothing worked.

After a long struggle, this is what I finally came up with: "Let people empty their cups." Allow me to explain. Imagine that you want to give me some fresh squeezed orange juice. However, my cup is full because it has been sitting on my desk for a while and it is filled with old, cold coffee. Before I can receive your orange juice, you have to let me empty my cup.

It's the same with information. If you want to tell me something important, I won't be able to listen to you until after I have my say. Metaphorically, I have to make room in my cup for your information.

When you have something important to say, it is imperative to let others speak *first*. Brake yourself because they will not listen to you until they have "emptied their cups" by getting their own concerns off their chests.

Leadership with a Twist of Yoga
principle to remember:

To Lead is to Listen

When Steve, the Texas businessman called, he said, "After I heard your speech, I called my dad and told him that we were going up there and let that guy empty his cup."

Father and son drove to the ranch. On the way, the son advised his dad, "No matter what he says, let him yak. Please don't butt in. Let him chew the fat as long as he wants to. We'll just sit and listen."

They arrived at the house, settled onto the neighbor's couch and without prompting the old rancher started talking. He told stories of the land, how his family had settled there and what had happened to them. For three hours he told his tales while the father and son sat listening.

When the old rancher finally stopped talking, they asked for the right of way. He granted it immediately. The businessman exclaimed, "For three *years* we had been telling him why we needed it, but we never convinced him. Three *hours* of listening and he gave us what we wanted!"

When you have something important to say, don't say it right away. Hold back. If you listen first, you will let people "empty their cups." Then, when it is your turn to speak, they will be able to take in your information.

You can use this with your family, you can use it with your staff, and you can use it with your banker, literally. I've tried this with many different kinds of people and it usually works. When you have something important to say or you need to ask for something – listen first.

In the story at the beginning of this chapter, when my co-worker talked about herself for fifty minutes, then stopped and asked, "What about you?" that was the pivotal moment. She had emptied her cup. I could have asked for something then, because at that instant she was open to me. With people like this, the moment passes quickly. So, don't wait. When the opportunity arrives, jump in.

Most people are busy planning what to say next even though they may appear to be listening. It isn't that their motives aren't pure. It is just that when they focus on the destination, and not the journey, they lose their sense of discovery.

Yoga instructor Mia Wigmore says that yoga helps her to empty her cup, making it easier to process information, wait for wisdom and clarity, and then let it go. Both yoga and listening are practices that help you to "be" and not "do." They help you to strengthen inner independence and feelings of self-worth which make a huge impact on the effect you have on others. You can't fake a good effect, but you can create one by listening.

Do you listen to naysayers?

Irma Colin was one of my mentors. I watched her raise millions of dollars for worthy causes in Los Angeles. One day the organizers of a small free medical clinic approached her for help. The clinic was in Venice, California, near the beach. They had a great need to attract doctors because, at that time, Venice was a low-income area with lots of people who couldn't afford medical care. The clinic had one doctor who volunteered one-half day each week. They needed at least one dozen doctors.

Skeptics told Irma, "It can't be done. You'll never find twelve doctors to volunteer." They laughed at her for trying, saying, "It's a long-standing problem. Doctors are busy. What makes you think you can change that?"

What would you do to solve the problem? It is similar to other situations you will face when you are in a leadership position. (Too much to do and too few resources.) If you listen to your doubts, succumb to the skeptics and agree that it can't be done, you'll be right. Irma, however, saw it in a different light.

Instead of seeing the need as a problem, Irma saw it as a challenge to be solved. A worthy challenge. She looked at the need (they needed more doctors.) Next, she looked at the community and got an idea. A lot of artists lived in Venice. They had converted the empty warehouses and broken-down storefronts into large studios. Venice had artists and needed doctors. How could Irma put the two together to benefit both? Voila! The Venice Art Walk was born.

Irma and a team of volunteers offered the artists a unique opportunity: They could show their work to a large, new audience. They agreed and opened their studios for tours. People from all over the city paid to meet the artists and visit the studios. The money went to the clinic. With lots of publicity, the event became a "happening." The Art Walk made the Venice Family Clinic famous. Suddenly, doctors wanted to volunteer there. When it began, the clinic had one doctor who donated one-half day a week. Later, the clinic grew to over 500 volunteer doctors, a multi-million-dollar budget and became one of the largest free clinics in the world.

When she began, Irma had no idea how to recruit doctors. But she didn't listen to those who said, "It can't be done." She asked, "What is the best way to do it?"

When you say, "It can't be done," your brain stops working. On the other hand, if you ask, "What is the best way to do it?" your brain goes to work to figure it out. By seeing your challenge as an opportunity even when you have no idea how it can be solved, you'll inspire people to rise to the occasion, be creative and accomplish way beyond your expectations.

CREATIVITY Exercise
How to turn *CAN'T* into *CAN*

Based on Irma's success, I created an exercise that I've since used with dozens of organizations. It helps you deal with reality as it is, not as you wish it would be. In this exercise, you use what you have to get what you need.

1. Make a list of what you have.
2. Make a list of what you need.
3. With your team, brainstorm various ways to put the two lists together.

For example: You have a lot of artists. You need doctors. How can you use what you have to create what you need?

With this exercise:

- You can be creative.
- You can combat skepticism.
- You can create buy-in.
- You can find new approaches to old problems.
- You can give people a chance to have a breakthrough and do something different.

On your list of what you have, you probably have something that other people want, something that has benefits to them. Venice had a lot of artists. Irma thought people would enjoy touring the artist studios. By offering something that people wanted, she turned the challenge into a success.

Many people only saw the broken-down storefronts. They looked at the original Venice Family Clinic and got discouraged by the large number of children in need of medical attention. Irma, however, didn't focus on the need, the scarcity. She focused on what they had. This insight inspired thousands of people, including artists, art lovers, and the much-needed doctors to get involved.

Another aspect of Irma's success was her enthusiasm. When you are honestly enthusiastic, people want to listen to you. Enthusiasm enables you to inspire cooperation. It warms the heart. If communication between workers and management is cold, your organization will fail to realize its full potential. Enthusiasm unifies people. Enthusiasm is a real force in society and particularly in business. Even the most well-organized company cannot succeed without it, so be enthusiastic. If you feel it, express it. The results can be magical.

For every problem there is a solution. Even if the solution is not apparent, it is there. Your challenge is to not listen to the naysayers. It takes work to remain positive until you find the solution. Negativity can blind you to opportunities. Something very valuable (like the artists in Venice) could be right under your nose and you won't see it.

After cutting off his own ear, the Dutch artist Van Gogh wrote to his brother, Theo, saying, "As a painter I shall never amount to anything. I'm absolutely sure of this."

Despite his enormous talent, the artist didn't profit from his own masterpieces. Still, they were masterpieces. His brother's widow thought they were valuable. She refused to give up and in her lifetime the paintings began to sell. Later, other people bought and sold Van Gogh's work for fortunes. Could the artist listening to his own negativity have been the impediment?

"As you think, so you become."

Upanishads

According to Newton's third law of motion, every action has an equal and opposite reaction. The exchange of energy keeps the universe in balance.

Bhavya Sharma, Assistant Professor of Chemistry at the University of Tennessee, Knoxville, has found this to be true in working with her students. She says, "Whatever I do has an effect. I have to serve as a leader, mentoring my students so they can become leaders. For example, it is easy to get caught up in lab work and forget to eat. So, I ask my students if they have had lunch. Are they drinking enough water? I've noticed that now my grad students ask others the same question. It is perpetuated by me being that way."

According to Newton, forces always come in pairs. (For every action, there is an equal and opposite reaction.) So, when objects or people interact with each other, they exert forces upon each other. These two forces are called action and reaction.

This may seem anathema to traditional management ideas, but if you put less force on someone, they will put less force into resisting you. When you follow what is good in yourself, there is an equal reaction in others. Not necessarily instantly. All things come in due time. But even your smallest self-improvement, will make an impact around you.

Another lesson we can learn from science that can be used in working with people is from Newton's first law of motion. It states that all objects will remain at rest or in a uniform state of motion unless an outside force acts on the system.

Professor Sharma explains, "Everything in the universe is in a state that does not want to change. It wants to remain the same to keep everything in balance. To perturb (or change) a system, you have to constantly add force to it, because the system wants to return to the original state."

She says, "You may think, 'I need to exercise but I don't have time.' You must get over the thought 'I don't have time,' because according to the first law of motion the universe is pulling you back to the original state. A change won't stay infinitely in the new state. So, to change permanently, you have to put work into it."

When you want to make a change that you know is right: persevere. Conflict is part of life. Twists and turns are part of the creative process. Remember this when others are doubting your direction or when people disappoint you or let you down. Are you strong enough to be gentle with their transgressions? Can you remember what is luminous in them? Adversity is necessary for growth, so can you be reasonable about small imperfections?

Creativity always includes a chaotic process which can be an annoyance, an obstruction, and it can even doom your endeavor. It can also be just the friction you need to polish your project into shiny brilliance. If you are a musician, you know it takes tension on guitar strings to make magnificent music.

The multiple possibilities at the beginning of a new situation create ambiguity. Don't let yourself be intimidated by the confusion. Ride out the storm. Amid the stress you won't have a clear perspective. Don't expect to. If you let the creative process unfold, later you will see that almost everything that happens can be used for a good purpose.

To be creative, you must be able to tolerate pain. Artistic processes require perseverance. And they take time. Can you ride it out? Can you remain true to your vision through the changes? Doubt can make you grab a quick solution. But is it the right solution? Impatience is dangerous in a creative project. If you can remain open to suggestions, and balanced through the tension, on your own day you will be believed. And if you aren't? Sometimes falling on your face can be the best teacher.

Do you believe that you can get what you need from what you have? If not, don't worry about it. Miracles occur every day. Just be open to the possibility. Why shouldn't a miracle happen for you?

Catherine Ertelt, was trying to sell a condominium in the Denver area during what she calls "a bust cycle." Foreclosures were rampant in Colorado at that time. Although she loved living there and the condo was in a beautiful location, a new job required her to move to another state so she needed to sell.

When she advertised the condo, there were hundreds of competing condominiums on the market. Friends were discouraging about her chances to find a buyer. Catherine says she tried not to listen, although it was hard because there were so many naysayers.

"I kept my attention on the reasons why I loved living there," she recalls. "The condo was located in the foothills. It was on a pond. It had a beautiful view. It looked across fields where I could hear horses running in the morning. I felt perfectly safe jogging there at night."

She purposely kept her focus on why she loved that condo. Note that she didn't lie to herself about it being easy. She just didn't listen to the people who said it was hard. She concentrated on what was good about the condo.

"The sale was fast," Catherine says. "Within one month I had a buyer. After the closing, the woman who bought it told me that she bought it for the duck pond."

Catherine refused to let other people's comments dissuade her from the benefits she knew about her condo. Years later, she used this same positive thinking technique on a job where she was a scheduler. She regularly had more work than she had people to do the work. When requests came in, she refused to say, "No one is available." Instead, she asked herself, "Who would like to do this?" Invariably, Catherine says a worker would walk in asking, "Do you have something for me to do?"

Practice not listening to negativity. Don't justify trying to do what is correct. Don't despair when it seems difficult. At the same time, be modest about your "positivity." Success won't come through arrogance, but through a more subtle persuasion. It is worth the effort because people lend a hand when you are positive. They give you their backing. A positive outlook is capable of softening hearts. Be positive (in an honest way) and you'll inspire people to be positive about you.

A famous sportscaster was asked to give professional advice to a young producer, just entering the sports television arena. His advice was, "Get to know all parts of the business, not just your small slice of the pie." Pushing for a meteoric rise to the top is not as likely to bring success as a clear vision of where you are going. The following technique will help you to do what the sportscaster suggests.

Want to rise up the ranks quickly? Use this listening technique to advance.

- First, ask others at your company to explain their jobs to you (and listen.)
- Second, go back to your desk and write down everything you can remember.
- Third, ask a co-worker to interpret the notes with you.

A lot of people understand the importance of steps one and two but they skip step three. (Most rely on themselves to interpret what they've heard.) Leaving out step three will lead to a long, slow process of coming to understand the culture. Including step three will help you to advance quickly.

Do you listen to warnings from your customers?

The YMCA of the Chesapeake in Maryland (where I used to belong) did a customer satisfaction survey. Only 36% of the members rated the Y as excellent. The next year, 56% rated it as excellent. That was a 20% jump in only one year.

To make this big jump, the Y asked their customers, "How are we doing?" Then they listened. Often, we are afraid to ask the question. Who knows what responses we will get? But if we don't ask, how will we know how to improve?

Robbie Gill, the CEO, was new at that time and wanted to make improvements. He says they focused on small things first. Did the front desk people listen? When he called in, he listened to how the staff answered the telephone. When he liked it, he'd say, "Thank you! That was a great way to answer."

After they listened to the members' comments and suggestions, the responses were posted for all to see and the YMCA made changes. The results: Members, volunteers, and donations increased, and the Y balanced its budget for the first time in 38 years! Since then, the organization has made huge leaps with over 90% of the county population participating. Their latest approval rating was 70% member satisfaction.

Most people think that to make a big improvement, you have to do something big. Not so. As illustrated by CEO Robbie Gill, sometimes you can make small changes and get big results.

Leadership usually involves some form of chaos. Don't be intimidated by the storm. Stress can prevent you from gaining a true perspective. Confusion can be annoying. It can also doom your endeavor. So, control a huge ambition and don't try to make too many changes quickly. Eventually, however, just as summer changes to fall, it will become clear that the time has arrived to make an important modification. When that happens, even if you are afraid of the consequences, do it, because if you don't make changes, your career will not progress.

Kerry LaRosa is an entrepreneur in Philadelphia. One of her major customers regularly ordered a lot of printing materials, brochures, signage, etc.

"This customer places large orders," Kerry says. "They also have high expectations and I pride myself on being able to deliver. I like to give exceptional customer service."

Over time, Kerry noticed that the customer's expectations became harder to meet. "There were tighter deadlines; they asked for more and more color corrections; and they were abrupt when they spoke to me," she says. "Still, I was delivering."

One day, they placed a huge order with a very tight deadline. They wanted it almost immediately. It was doable if they delivered the files on-time as promised. They didn't. Kerry received the design work only two days before the printing was supposed to be completed. Still, she managed to have it ready for delivery on the due date. It was a Friday and the day of a huge ice, snow, sleet, hail storm.

Kerry says, "I could not find a driver on such a day. The roads were treacherous. Being the superstar that I am, I decided to make the delivery myself. What normally would take one hour, took three hours. But the delivery was made and I was relieved to be done with it."

On the way back to her office, Kerry received a telephone call from her customer. Several pieces of signage were missing. Kerry was incredulous. This couldn't be happening. She pulled off to the side of the road to make phone calls. After 45 minutes of going back and forth on the phone, she discovered that the files had been named incorrectly in the rush. Despite all of this, Kerry delivered the completed job on Monday morning.

Looking back, she says, "That day in the snowstorm, sitting in the car on the side of the road I felt utterly drained. A wave of resentment washed over me. The customer had become more and more demanding. But I had let it happen. I had allowed my so-called excellent customer service to go too far. It was sobering. I knew that this could not happen again, even if it meant losing the customer."

The next week, Kerry called the company's marketing director and talked about what had happened. Only silence came from the other end of the call. Kerry was afraid that she'd lost the huge account. Time passed. Then, two weeks later the next order came in. Along with the order, they sent a spreadsheet with the exact details. They allowed plenty of time, even adding two extra days for production. Kerry says, "Best of all, there was a positive shift in the way they spoke to me."

Never go against your gut. Listen to the warning signs, no matter how subtle they appear. If you don't, what seems like a twitch can turn into a tornado. When you agree to a decision that you don't feel right about, if you let it go (as Kerry did) down the road a ripple can become a tidal wave. Fortunately for Kerry, she spoke up and kept her customer. She also kept her health and her self-respect.

Yoga is about balance and stability. Kerry realized that she needed these in her personal life in order to thrive in her business. By speaking up, Kerry demonstrated one of the most essential principles of yoga, "dharma," which essentially means to be ethical, to do the right thing, including toward yourself. By speaking up, she did the right thing. When she aligned herself with the "dharma" of the situation, Kerry's client reciprocated and continued to work with her.

"A good listener is not only popular everywhere, but after a while he gets to know something."

Wilson Mizner

When do you listen to feedback?

Senior Manager of Employee Development at CPS Energy in Texas, Elizabeth Ackley has a vivid memory of receiving some valuable feedback when she first started working at her company.

"Richard had worked there 23 years and I was new on the job. He took me under his wing helping me understand the culture," she says, "I was nervous at my first presentation but I made it through the ordeal, and actually felt great. People congratulated me on a job well done. As the room slowly emptied out, Richard lingered."

The conversation went something like this:

He: Good job.

She: Thank you.

He: May I give you feedback?

She: Yes.

He: You were nervous, weren't you? I could tell because when you are nervous you flip your hair. I know you are smart. When we watch you flipping your hair, it undermines your credibility. I recommend that you wear your hair tied back when you make a presentation.

Elizabeth thought she had done a good job, so she was embarrassed by his feedback. She says, "Before he said it, I was riding on cloud 9 and he knew that. It took an amazing amount of courage on his part to tell me the truth. Without that feedback, I wouldn't have known. Richard also gave me a solution, which was priceless."

Elizabeth thinks the secret to good feedback is to be very, very specific and offer a fix (as Richard did.) She described another example of feedback that she witnessed at a different company where she worked early in her career:

Elizabeth's friend, Sandy, accepted a promotion into a new position that catapulted her to assisting top-tier management. Immediately she was working with all of the senior leadership team. One day her co-worker, Patricia, asked, "Do you want some feedback?"

Sandy: Yes.

Patricia: Everybody thinks you are only working here for the money and the prestige.

Taken aback, Sandy asked: Everybody? The customers? My team partners?

Patricia: Three people said so.

It was such a painful experience for Sandy that it hurled her out of her new job. She made a lateral move, back to where she had worked before the promotion.

Elizabeth says, "This is not feedback. It is mean-spirited. Instead of being helpful, it tapped into Sandy's fear. Either Patricia wanted to make Sandy better and didn't know how to give feedback. Or, she is a bully and wanted dominance."

If you want people to listen to your feedback, Elizabeth suggests separating DO from WHO. What did the person do? Elizabeth flipped her hair. Richard talked about a specific action.

His feedback was timely. It had just happened. Also, his advice was kind. He took ownership, offering his own thoughts, not gossip. He didn't say, "Everyone thinks this." It was something she could change. You did X. The result was Y. The solution is Z.

The cruel co-worker made a broad, sweeping, accusatory comment. When Sandy probed for details, Patricia didn't give any specifics. This is disempowering because there is no action the person can take to improve. Sandy was left wondering, "How do I change their minds about me?"

Listening can be with your eyes, too. Richard observed Elizabeth. He started with a commitment to her success. He wanted her to improve and be better. This kind of feedback is rooted in trust. It is strong, but it doesn't wound. When feedback is rooted in trust, it can be listened to.

These two stories demonstrate "dharma." Richard gave his feedback in an ethical, constructive, "dharmic" way. Patricia gave feedback in a hurtful, nonconstructive "un-dharmic" way.

Often, the desire to be helpful turns into pressing ourselves on others. For the person receiving the feedback, it takes courage to listen. If you are the one giving feedback, hold back until you are sure that they trust you. Delay until their resistance has given way. Until then, remain open-minded about them and wait for the right time to have an effect.

Executive Producer Makario Sarsozo was introduced to yoga by his mother when he was a child. He says, "It is good to listen to feedback but don't let it own you. It is always filtered through the other person's life experiences. So, listen, and also trust yourself. Both giving and receiving feedback has made me be keenly aware of my influence on others. Our words have a ripple effect that can be beneficial and help shape their future or create a catastrophe that tilts them into chaos."

When you ask for feedback, do you listen to the answer?

"Sometimes a two-way dialogue can make the situation ten times better," says Ashok Moore of WWE and previously a producer at ESPN. "Who knows better than your own team members the values, priorities, and culture of your project? A lot of the best ideas are right in front of you, if you listen."

When Ashok first started at ESPN over a dozen years ago, the parent company Disney conducted a survey asking the employees for feedback about their day to day experience of working for the company. One thing that people complained about was not having a consistent schedule.

"I would start at 4 am in the morning one day, and the next week I would start work at 5:30 pm in the afternoon. The inconsistent hours made it difficult to make plans outside of work," Ashok says, "I loved working at ESPN but I also needed to establish a life independent of it."

The survey revealed that Ashok was not the only employee with this concern and the Disney company responded, essentially saying, "We've heard you. We are going to change it." And they did. The benefit turned out to be not only for the employees, but for the company, too. Afterwards, ESPN experienced increased productivity and better creativity.

Ashok says, "When the hours were jumping all over the place, so were your teammates. You worked with different people every day. This impacted all levels of employees, including the anchors and the producers. When the hours became steady, you worked with the same team mates regularly which built camaraderie. And it built a dynamic establishment."

In the company's defense, it was growing quickly at the beginning and there were many needs to be filled hurriedly. But people were hurting. After the survey, the company changed. Later, when new employees questioned the value of the yearly survey, Ashok told them this story. He says, "It's an example of when a company did listen and it improved things."

Do you listen to your intuition?

David Hetzel was the lead attorney in a case for a large corporation. The client he represented was shifting from one internet provider to another and had to terminate a relationship with the first provider. If he didn't win, the loss would cost David's client millions of dollars.

The two sides raced to be first to file their lawsuit. David says, "I filed in Delaware, and they immediately filed their lawsuit in Texas. Because of this, we needed a quick mandatory injunction." David couldn't wait for the court's normal timeline. Late on a Friday afternoon he went into Federal Court in Delaware and asked for a ruling on an emergency basis. The judge listened carefully to what David said but wasn't prepared to enter the order he requested. He temporarily denied the request and told David to come back the next week.

It was a huge setback for David's client. Things got even worse that Friday afternoon when the other side was successful in Texas. The Texas court issued a quick injunction favoring the opponent. This meant David's client would have to pay both providers at a cost of millions.

"Late Friday night," David remembers, "I was at my hotel in Delaware and had to call my client to give him the bad news. He was General Counsel of the company and a man I had immense respect for. He was one of those icons that appear

"From knowledge known as Pratibha (intuition) everything becomes known."

Yoga Sutra III:33

sometimes in professional life that you look up to and you'd like to be like."

David got him on the phone. He says, "I remember sitting there on the bed in my hotel room with the phone in one ear, my head sagging, telling him the horrible news."

The General Counsel replied, "This is the worst day of my professional life."

David says, "To hear him say that, I was absolutely crushed. In every case, you care about your cause; you care about doing the thing your client needs. I felt awful already, but when those words came from him – of all people – they cut like a knife."

The General Counsel then said, "I want *you* to tell the news to the client. Talk to the Chief Executive Officer tomorrow. You tell him what happened."

"I didn't sleep much that night," David remembers, "Early on Saturday morning I flew home. As I was driving from the airport I was thinking and praying, what was I going to say? How was I going to explain the situation? What could I do to calm their fears? I was trying to get centered when, suddenly, it was as if someone literally whispered into my ear. The voice said, *'All you have to do is show up and tell the truth. God will take care of the rest.'*"

David felt a huge weight lift off his shoulders. He knew it was true. The best thing he could do was show up and tell the truth. He felt enormously relieved. Suddenly lighthearted, he began singing in the car.

"Soon after that I got on the phone with their executive team, the General Counsel, the Chief Executive and the Chief Operating Officer. I told them what happened," David says.

"You told them everything, even your prayer?!" I exclaimed when he told me the story.

He laughed, "I didn't tell them about the voice in my head. I told them about the events that had taken place. Then, in clear and unequivocal terms I told them what we were going to do about it. I did it in a very compelling way, without rehearsal, just speaking the words as they came to me."

When David finished, the Chief Executive said, "That sounds fine. We'll go that way. Let me know what happens."

By the next Monday morning at 8:30 am, the Texas injunction was dissolved. David had flown to Dallas, appeared before the judge and explained why the restraining order he had entered was not justified. The judge agreed. He then flew to Delaware and by Wednesday night, David's client had the mandatory injunction entered in their favor in federal court. The case had taken a 180-degree turn. It was a spectacular reversal. The case settled and David's clients saved millions of dollars.

Listen to your intuition. You have the solutions. You may not know it, but you do. David listened to his own inner voice of wisdom. By trusting his intuition, he opened himself up to additional possibilities.

If you get into a situation similar to David Hetzel's predicament (and you may) in which there are no obvious solutions and you fear blame will fall on you, there is no need to become defensive. Don't pretend that you have all the answers. Instead, trust your intuition. If an answer comes to you from inside – listen!

Suppose an answer doesn't come from inside? Then pay attention to what comes to you on the outside. A wise teacher can take many forms. It can be an inner prompting or the voice of experience. It may be a book of wisdom. Your answer may also come from a friend, a supervisor, a business advisor, or anyone to whom you turn for advice.

Most of us have a strong tendency to swing towards justification, even retaliation, when we feel forced into an impossible situation. Please don't take this route. It will prevent you from hearing good advice. It will prevent people from giving their opinions. If you are defensive, others will be resistant to you. If you try to vindicate yourself, help won't come because it drives people away.

Learning only happens when your heart is open and humble. So, again, listen. A joyous leader doesn't have all of the answers. A joyous leader recognizes when she needs help. Accept your need for help, call for it, and then be open. As in David Hetzel's case, answers arrive in amazing ways. All you have to do is listen.

Trust your intuition!

"There comes a point where the mind takes a leap – call it intuition or what you will – and comes out upon a higher plane of knowledge but can never prove how it got there. All great discoveries have involved such a leap."

Einstein

Yoga Wisdom
Dharma & Detachment

Two important concepts from yoga that will be beneficial to you in leadership are dharma and detachment.

Dharma loosely means to be ethical and "to do the right thing." People often ask, "What is my great work?" If you do the work in front of you greatly, ethically, it will lead you to your great work.

Dharma is about living the life you were meant to live. It can be as simple as not comparing yourself to the person next to you. One of the most influential treatises in Eastern philosophy, the Bhagavad Gita says, "It is better to do your own dharma even imperfectly, than someone else's dharma perfectly." For instance, an actor on a stage has to play her own part, not someone else's part. In the same way, in your career and your life, when you are the boss, be the boss. When you are a parent, be the parent. If you embrace your current fate, you'll gain the strength and courage that you need for what lies ahead.

Through dharma the weak can overcome the strong, according to the Upanishads which are a collection of philosophical texts written in India about 700 BC. The same point has been made throughout the ages in many traditions. It is illustrated beautifully by the Bible story of David and Goliath. A small boy defeats a larger, stronger, gigantic opponent because he does the right thing.

"Dharma destroys those who destroy it. Dharma protects those who protect it."

Motto of the National Law School of India

Yogis believe that when you do the right thing, dharma protects. When you don't, dharma destroys. Even though Goliath had all the brute force he needed, he was not doing the right thing and David, only a small boy with a sling shot, destroyed him.

When David, the attorney, thought that he had lost the lawsuit, he did the right thing (the "dharmic" thing) by not justifying and making excuses for himself. He accepted responsibility and, in the end, he was protected. Elizabeth's story shows how to give and receive feedback dharmically, correctly. Kerry, whose biggest customer mistreated her, had to do the right thing for herself even if it meant losing the client. Bradley's story (that is coming up) is another example of dharma. He had to fire employees which was the necessary thing to do, even when it wasn't easy.

Everyday leaders grapple with issues of values, virtues, and ethics. They are constantly faced with moral dilemmas including grievances, anger, feeling hard and proud, overconfidence about being right, or stepping outside the correct limits. Strong emotions lock us into battle with ourselves and others. When this comes up, ask yourself, "What is my dharma? What is the right thing to do?"

"Don't be encumbered by past history.
Go off and do something wonderful."

Robert Noyce, Intel

Detachment:

The Sanskrit word for detachment is "Vairagya" which means release from desire and consequently from suffering. Being attached to results can be painful and disappointing. Detachment calms the passions. It helps you be in the moment, which is the only way to truly be creative. It doesn't mean we forget what we have learned from the past or abandon our wishes for the future, we just recognize their transitory nature.

Practicing detachment helps immensely when we are trying to influence people. It is a brief period of time when they are receptive to us. When that moment wanes, let go. Detach and wait. If you keep pushing, you'll push people away.

Patanjali's yoga sutra 1:12 teaches, "You are responsible for your work. Not for the fruits of your work." You can control your actions. You cannot control the results of your actions. If you can do your duty, but not become fixated on the results, your life will be more creative and less hectic.

Saraswati Clere, an award-wining documentary filmmaker, who owns Yogakula Wellness Center in Berkeley, California says, "As a yogi and also a business owner, you have an opportunity to use the teachings and practices to support the business. Yoga provides a great foundation to ride the ups and downs and makes the whole journey much more fulfilling and joyful."

"During the tough times my yoga practice keeps me steady and enables me to find new ways to grow the business," she says. At one point her business took a huge setback. She recalls, "It was disappointing, but it forced me to change my business model. When I did, it started growing back better than before."

Saraswati says, "Detachment and self-awareness give you the ability to turn inside and do what is needed right now. It gives you the strength to remember that when something closes, there is something new coming. That's when you have to be careful and clear about your intention. If you have a clear vision of what can be, you'll be able to walk the distance to reach it."

Dharma and detachment may seem like opposites, but they are two parts of one whole. If you do the right thing and then detach from expecting certain results, you'll be happy immediately ... and successful eventually. The dualistic nature of the universe is something that yoga helps us overcome. The interplay of opposites is deeply rooted in yoga. Remember that in Sanskrit, "yoga" means unite or yoke. Through unity, seeming contradictions are reconciled to create wholeness and balance.

An understanding of yoga brings awareness and sheds light on a situation whether it is stress in your body or an issue with co-workers. It is said that the mind can travel a million miles in the blink of an eye. Yoga brings you back to the present moment. When your mind is muddled or your thoughts are wandering, you can't listen. When you are in the midst of an emotional upheaval, detachment helps you relax. Detachment does not mean to sweep things under the rug. If you do that, the alienation grows. It doesn't go away until there is understanding, which usually requires listening to others and to your own heart.

Listening with detachment means listening without responding emotionally. When we get angry it is often because we are holding onto how we think something should be – our pride, our righteousness, our expectations, wanting people and situations to be something that they are not. Detachment creates contentment, which makes it possible to serve others without depriving yourself.

To serve others, never purposely put yourself in a weak position. Too many leaders, in an attempt to appear humble, give away their power. Gentle words can be strong, especially when spoken from the heart. However, gentleness is worthless if dispensed with apprehension. Detachment makes it easier to be gentle and strong at the same time.

Bradley Horowitz, VP Product at Google, says, "The job of the leader is not to be loved and admired. It is to do what needs to be done. This goes against a natural inclination to want to be liked and popular." He advises, "Play the long game. Do what needs to be done or you don't deserve the title of CEO or any title, for that matter."

When he was running his startup, Bradley had to lay off dozens of people and sometimes he had to fire people. "It is never pleasant," he says, "Many people got angry and reactive in those meetings. It was hard to hold steady in the wake of their anger or heartbreak." However, in the ensuing years almost all of them came back and said things like, "Even though it was hard at the time, afterwards I went to the South Pacific and changed my life." Or, "I got the perfect job, so it was the best thing ever."

Bradley learned that, "If it isn't working for the company, then no way is it working for the individual. As a leader, you have the moral obligation to liberate them. Realizing this emboldened me. Now I look for the mutual best interest – what is best for the company, for me and for them."

From the yoga wisdom point of view, the only way to know if we have done the right thing is by the results. For this reason, when you find yourself in a confusing moment, remember one thing: dharma protects. Do the right thing and then detach from trying to manipulate the results. You'll be protected.

Do you listen to your own truth? Only when you are loyal to your own truth can you be loyal to others…and then earn their loyalty. You can't command it. You can't legislate it. You can't contrive or force loyalty. People may comply for a while, but not

"I have finally forgiven myself for not being Beethoven."

Neil Diamond

for long. When you are loyal to what you know is good, people will follow you willingly.

Mina Azizi has a PhD in Industrial/Organizational Psychology. Mina's company, AltaMed Health Services, offers a weekly yoga class during the lunch break that she says is a time for renewal and regeneration. One day, while doing the pigeon pose, she had an "ah-hah." Mina realized how much tension we hold in our bodies. She says, "I felt sheer joy at getting in touch with that tension. I always heard that – now I was experiencing it. I realized I had been ignoring my body. Not being kind to it. When I got in touch with the tension, I could release it."

In another lunchtime yoga class, Mina had a realization about the mind-body connection. "I thought it was either / or. For the first time I realized they are connected. They both affect your balance. It was a powerful insight for me."

Mina and three of her co-workers on the training team opted to take the yoga classes together. She says, "We all have office jobs. We sit a lot. There's a mystique to yoga – thinking you have to look a certain way. But our classes are restorative. Not too sweaty. We turn off our brains and relax." When I asked her why more people don't do it, she said, "The idea of leaving your desk seems radical. Work is a race. Most people want to grind it out. But most of us sit too long. It affects our posture. We need to develop balance."

Mina says, "When I feel anxious or self-critical, I use the yoga class to get in touch with myself and turn off judgment. Just by addressing the challenge, you exhibit a new awareness and gain a fresh perspective."

Mina's story is an example of how detachment improves flexibility. Gandhi said that his commitment was to truth, not to consistency. To others he may have seemed inconsistent when

he appeared to contradict himself, but imagine a river flowing toward the sea. Sometimes it goes right and sometimes left. It is consistent when you are looking at the big picture.

Be like the river and its water. A river spills over every cliff no matter how steep. When it comes upon an obstacle, it flows around. At a hole, it fills it up and moves on. This is not inconsistency. It is flexibility. People learn from the mistakes they make. Leaders grow strong from obstacles overcome. Don't judge yourself harshly when you make a mistake. Flow with it. Success lies with those who endure. In your mind, imagine the river moving around obstacles and carry on.

We gain power through detachment. (Doing the right thing and then not worrying about what others think of us.) We lose power through attachment. ("I need your approval.") The only way you can fail is if you quit or you let yourself be held back by doubt and fear.

In nature, the end of a cycle is also the starting point of the beginning. Seven days bring the start of a new week, four weeks a new month, twelve months a new year, etc. You will always be given a new beginning, another chance, a new lease on life, if you can be flexible. Flexibility makes it easier to listen to others, to warnings, and to your intuition.

The Twist

Bharadvajasana

Bharadvajasana – The Twist

Again, this is important: Not all yoga poses are suitable for everyone. Be gentle on yourself. More important than listening to the instructions is to listen to your own body. Be careful.

Twists make you more flexible, mentally and physically. Twists are designed to restore the spine's natural range of motion, stimulating circulation, improving digestion and focus. Some say the twist is soothing to the soul. Mentally, it helps restore harmony and prepares you for the future with new insights and understandings.

As a leader, your career will be full of twists and turns. If you are flexible you can forgive what you have begrudged and rebuild what you may have torn down. Practicing twists helps you see things with a fresh perspective.

- Sit on a chair with your feet and knees parallel.
- Place your left hand on the chair back and the right hand on your left knee as you inhale and lift the spine.
- Exhale and turn left, pulling with the left hand and pushing with the right for leverage.
- Focus your twist from the bottom of the spine first; head and neck last. Lifting is more important than how much you turn. Just like in your career, you'd rather go upward than sideways.
- Twists improve the spine's natural range of motion and stimulate circulation. When you release the twist, fresh blood flows into the internal organs.
- Repeat on the other side placing your right hand on the chair back, left hand on the right knee, breathing in, lifting, and then breathing out as you twist.

Gems to Remember

Empty Your Cup
Texas Rancher and the Right of Way

What You Have & What You Need
Artists and Doctors

To Lead is to Listen
As You Think, So You Become

Keeping the Universe in Balance
Actions and Equal Reactions

Listening to Customers, Feedback & Intuition
Supportive vs. Destructive

Dharma & Detachment
Do the Right Thing

Bharadvajasana
The Twist and Flexibility

Exercise for Success

1. The Texas Businessman and his father: What changed that helped them get what they wanted? Can you apply it to your work? How?
2. The Family Clinic: What could you learn from Irma and the creativity exercise?
3. Newton's third law of motion: If you put less force on someone, they will put less force into resisting you. To apply this to your organization, what will you do?
4. The condo owner who resisted negativity: How will you deal with naysayers in your business?
5. The YMCA and ESPN listening to their customers and employees: If you ask for input, and you don't like the answer, how will you handle it?
6. When and how do you listen to your intuition? In what other ways do you listen?

What is a human being's greatest support?

Chapter Three: How to Win Support

Nobody ever stopped him in the street to say,
'My dear Scrooge, how are you?'

What will you do if you find yourself in the following situation?

You've become isolated like Scrooge. Your employees don't trust you. They think that managers and employees have different objectives and different loyalties. They believe you are polar opposites like fire and water. They don't perceive that by following *your* lead, they can achieve what *they* want.

At the same time, you need their support. You can't carry a big load if you have no assistance. You can't lead if no one is following. What will you do if you find yourself unsupported (perhaps even hindered) by the people who should be coming to your aid?

A wise teacher of yoga posed this question to a student over a thousand years ago: *What is a human being's greatest support?* I have asked the same question to many audiences. Their answers to me indicate that support comes to human beings from numerous sources: money, parents, friends, family, property, the earth, religion, health. Can you think of others?

The wise teacher gave only one answer: *A human being's greatest support is gratitude.*

When I first heard this statement, I didn't believe it. How could something as concrete as *support* be reliant on something as ephemeral as *gratitude?* Also, I didn't know if the teacher meant *receiving* gratitude or *giving* gratitude? Or, could it be both?

I met John Frieda on a bus in India. People often share their stories on long bus trips and John shared his story with me.

At age 17, John Frieda became the assistant to Mr. Leonard, a renowned hair stylist in London who became world famous for creating an ultra-short haircut for the super-thin model, Twiggy. Mr. Leonard's styles were featured regularly in Vogue magazine.

According to John, Mr. Leonard was a genius. John says, "I wanted to be the best assistant he ever had. My goal was that he would never have to ask me for anything. Standing next to him in the salon, I wanted to know exactly what he wanted every time he put his hand out. It became like a dance. My eyes never left his hands from 9 am to 6 pm."

Many people working with a mentor – or acting as an assistant – are dominated by desire and fear. Desire to look good and the fear of not being good enough. Neither will ever bring a positive result. On the other hand, keeping an open mind awakens potential. John wanted to be what his teacher needed, to be the best assistant, to give the best service. That opened John to receive the wisdom that Mr. Leonard had to offer.

Later, John Frieda opened his own salons in cities around the world. As an entrepreneur, he applied what he learned from Mr. Leonard plus what he learned from his own father. John's father had a simple philosophy: "There are two kinds of people in this world, givers and takers. Make sure you are a giver."

When I asked John how he applied his father's advice to the salon business, he said, "It is simple. I wanted every client to receive the best haircut ever. I didn't focus on the money. What mattered was doing it brilliantly. Money is a byproduct. If you don't give the best that you have to give, even if you get money, you'll be miserable."

Today, John Frieda's hair products are sold worldwide. When he reminisces about the advice he received from his mentor and his father, John says, "To this day, I am totally grateful to them."

Giving and receiving are inextricably two parts of one whole like east and west, earth and sky, leaders and followers. In the same way, giving and receiving *gratitude* are complements, not opposites. Again, it is about balance. In John Frieda's example, if you take money but don't give your best, you will feel incomplete.

When I was a young manager, a group of us were asked, "Which do you prefer: To give orders or take orders?" To me, it was the same thing. I reported to a supervisor who gave orders to me. Then I conveyed those orders to the people who reported to me.

The follower and the leader are equal, like the parts of a circle, because you can't have one without the other. It is a 50/50 partnership. Without night there is no day. Without winter there is no spring. One sacrifices itself, surrenders, and then let's go so that the universe can flourish. As the leader, if we succeed and then think that we did it all by ourselves, nothing will thrive.

In the same circular way, misunderstanding is a prelude to understanding. So, give people the space to err. When you are at odds with those that work with you, try appreciating their circumstances. It may require you to do something that appears to take you away from your goal. At the same time, it could bring you full circle, so that you can receive the results that you were wishing for.

"It is in giving that we receive."

Saint Francis of Assisi

Here's an example:

Bonnie Callens had a dilemma. She needed more time. When she was a successful wealth advisor, she had created a thriving career. Because Bonnie was accomplished at researching investments for her clients, her business did well. Still, she had a dilemma. She needed more time. If only her staff would take on more responsibility.

At first, Bonnie thought the solution was to hire more help, and yet, how could she possibly manage more staff members? The ones that she had took up all of her spare time. Every moment that wasn't spent with a client, was spent putting out fires or dealing with a staff member's troubles.

The hassle of staff squabbles can turn anyone into a big, bad boss which is why some entrepreneurs make the conscious choice not to expand their businesses. Bonnie recalls, "I thought all the service should go to the clients. I was always serving the investors, but with my staff, they were supposed to serve me."

Then Bonnie attended one of my *Joy of Leadership* trainings. She says, "One great thing I got from it is that, as the leader, your staff needs to be served, too." After that, she started sitting down with the person and saying, "I've noticed you're not quite yourself today. What's going on?"

"The responses were excellent," she comments, "Usually I found out something big was going on that I had no idea about. Often there was something I could do to help, but even if I couldn't, expressing it changed the whole atmosphere. I always did this with my clients but I hadn't extended it to my staff."

A turning point came when Bonnie asked one young, single mother, "What can I do to help?" She found out that the woman was under a lot of stress at home so Bonnie offered her a choice of three stress relieving activities. One selection was a massage.

"Love is not only for your growth, but also your pruning."

Kahlil Gibran in *The Prophet*

"It turned out that she'd never had a massage in her whole life," Bonnie exclaims, "She thought it was the most wonderful thing I could have done for her and it turned her whole attitude around." Bonnie was amazed when such a simple gesture changed the atmosphere in the office, too.

It is not mysterious talent that qualifies you for a leadership position. More often, it is your simplest gifts like your compassion or your ability to allow disturbing events to become beneficial. An unsettling incident can force you to find a better way and look at things from a fresh perspective. Adversity can make you shed rigidity and reexamine old ideas. It can make you grow and see wonderfully workable ways to solve a problem.

Success is a habit. Alternatively, failure is largely the result of bad habits. If you succumb to saying, "Poor me, my employees don't support me," you could spend years resenting, blaming, and complaining about them. Instead, create the new habit of attracting support by practicing gratitude.

You can close a gap between yourself and other people by expressing gratefulness. It eliminates feelings of lack, loneliness, and separation. It works like a magnet drawing people close. It helps you bring competitive people together. It influences a sad situation in a hidden, dynamic way causing those who have erred to change their point of view.

The practice of gratitude can make you feel like you've been given another chance; a new lease on life. It brings you back to the present. It helps you forgive. The power of gratitude is like the power of love. The more you give it away, the more you have. Gratitude attracts love, and love can do anything. It makes it possible to judge without being judgmental; to recognize the underlying fears and wounds that cause good people to make bad decisions. With gratitude, we are able to put the shortcomings of others into perspective.

3 Ways to Win Support

You will win support when:

1. You learn how to work with imperfect people.
2. You allow the whole team to share credit for your success.
3. You are generous with your appreciation.

What do you do when people are driving you crazy and there is no way that you could appreciate them? How do you release people from your rigid expectations? Resentment is a burden on us, not them. Policing the behavior of other people takes a lot of time and energy and rarely, if ever, results in the other person changing. We absolutely cannot change someone else. We can only change our self.

This practice helps me when I feel resentful:

1. Spot the resentment in myself. Recognize it. Name it.
2. Experience the feeling. Actually, ask myself, "Where in my body do I feel it?"
3. Acknowledge that it is just a feeling. Avoid going into a long story about how it came about. Focus on the feelings. (I feel tension in my stomach. My lips are pursed, etc.) People remember stories forever, but they don't hold onto feelings very long. The more you can ignore the story and focus on the feeling, the faster it will go away. The more you repeat the story, the longer it lasts.
4. Picture it like an ocean wave rolling out to sea, and watch it go. This doesn't mean it is gone forever. Like the ocean waves, it will come again. Then you repeat the practice.

What this exercise does for me is take the focus off of blaming the other person, and brings it back to something I can actually change, my own feelings. There is a Tibetan Buddhist practice called "Tonglen" that is similar. "Tonglen" means giving and receiving.

I can't change the other person, but I can change my own behavior. It is not easy, but it is doable. Working with my feelings this way helps me to be kind toward myself, which makes it easier to be kind to others.

John Frieda and Bonnie Callens created lucky breaks for themselves with gratitude. Bonnie gave her appreciation, changed the atmosphere in her office and then had more time. John built his business on a foundation of gratitude and became extremely successful.

- To receive gratitude, give your support.
- To receive support, give your gratitude.

Researchers Robert Simmons and Michael McCullough in their long-term study "Research Project on Gratitude and Thankfulness" found that people with a strong disposition toward gratitude are rated as more generous by their peers.

For Great Results...

Results matter. In the intense, high-powered, mostly male-dominated world of technology, a young single mother started with nothing and built her firm into a multimillion-dollar success story. Because of her own history, she is sensitive to the fact that her employees have lives outside of the office. She has a reputation for being a nourishing boss. She's also known to be demanding.

She tells her employees, "I'll listen to your situation and issues, and then you get the job done. If you don't perform, nothing else matters."

I remember a wonderful supervisor who hired me, then wouldn't let me dig into the job. I was raring to go and happy to have the new position but became confused and frustrated when she didn't give me enough to do.

"It's not enough that we do our best;
sometimes we have to do
what is required."

Sir Winston Churchill

Why do you think my supervisor did that? I was afraid that she didn't trust me. Or, worse, she thought I was not capable. What do you think? Why would she hire me and then not give me any responsibility?

Weeks went by while she worked and I watched. I didn't understand it at the time, but later realized that she was training me. I was not ready to manage big jobs, but I was watching big jobs being accomplished. Later, she taught me to train a new employee in my own department the same way by letting the new person shadow me and watch how I did the work. I found this to be more valuable than an official "training" for getting a new employee up and running.

How to Teach a Task

Too many times, when teaching a task, the teacher explains it over and over again. The student will learn much faster if you "show and then *don't* tell."

1. Do the task while your new assistants watch and make their own notes.
2. The next day, you watch while they do the work themselves reading from their notes. Of course, they'll make mistakes. Here's your challenge: Don't jump in and explain it again. Don't do it for them. Hold back. Don't "do." Just watch and be there to answer questions. They'll learn much faster if you can be patient, hold back and let them struggle. If you keep repeating the instructions, you'll slow down their learning process.
3. Only after they've completed the task do you step in and make necessary adjustments while they make changes to their notes. For the next three times, be available while they work. Not to instruct. Not to watch or hover over them. Just be nearby in case they stumble.

Doug Keller is an advanced hatha yoga teacher based in Washington D.C. who teaches all over the world. He is known for his therapeutic approach. Doug says, "Leadership from a yogic point of view has nothing to do with pretense. It is not so much leading as resonating. When you give instruction based on a personal experience, there is no need to project an image of bravado. Students get it. On the other hand, the one-size-fits-all approach will often lead to disaster."

Doug says, "People in my classes today are looking for more than just exercise. They are happy when they discover that they are strong enough to be gentle, and that all it takes is a small shift in perspective to realize it."

How to Delegate - Three L's

Delegate does not mean dump. Delegate means to empower, to entrust. Unfortunately, when most people say they want to delegate, they actually mean that they have taken on too much and want to get it off their plates and onto someone else's. It becomes a child's game of hot potato.

Why would anyone want to take on your burden? On the other hand, if the project is exciting, rewarding and fun, who wouldn't want to join in?

The next time you want to delegate, consider this: People aren't looking for ways to give up their time, but they are looking for ways to enrich their lives. Question yourself, "What is valuable about this project? Where's the joy? What drew you to it in the beginning?" Instead of asking them to do something that you don't want to do, offer an opportunity. Then use the Three L's to delegate.

1. Look for Good People

You don't want people to be growling through their tasks. You want people who will gleefully participate. Pay attention at meetings. Stand off to the side and see who is energetic in one direction or another versus who just wants to get through it.

Cub Scout leader Steven Gay says, "If you are in charge of the yearly camp-out, you'll find that some people really like to camp and some people really don't like to camp. The goal is not to force the people who don't like to camp into camping. The goal is a high-quality program. So, pick individuals who are enthusiastic about camping and it will go off like clockwork."

2. Listen to Them

Mary Castleberry has recruited a legion of volunteers for her church. She says, "Learn what people need from you before you try to delegate to them. By listening first, you learn what they like to do and what they want to do. Then delegate things to them that they like and want to do."

3. Let Them Shine

Give credit to others. Steven Gay says, "It makes them feel more important and gives them a feeling of fulfillment. Of course, when they look good, it makes you look good too. In the meantime, it frees you up to concentrate on organizing the whole project."

Leadership with a Twist of Yoga
principle to remember:

To Lead is to Appreciate

How do you turn reluctant employees into willing participants?

Traditionally, asking employees to do extra work fails. By "extra" I mean in addition to their normal duties. They may reluctantly agree, but only half-heartedly and then look for excuses not to participate. When he was an IBM Project Manager Charles Carrington says, "On average, these 'extra' projects have a 70% failure rate." Charles Carrington has a 70% success rate. What is the secret to the ones that succeed?

"It's a challenge to create a team where each person is basically taking on an extra part-time job," says Carrington. "In this situation, the best thing to do is to create something that they would volunteer for. When you do that, you create a more effective team."

All over the world there are millions of people who offer their time, for free, to causes that they believe in. Through their offering they receive something back. They see a change that they believe is *beneficial*. They get *satisfaction* in helping a worthy cause. They share the *camaraderie* of like-minded people.

It is a basic human need to want your life to count. People want to do a good job. They want to be of service. Carrington understands this and uses it to create his 70% success rate. Basically, his secret is this: Treat your team members as highly valued volunteers.

"When creating a team of volunteers in a business environment," says Carrington, "it is essential that you show the people on your team the benefits to *them*."

When you want people to participate willingly, don't talk about how hard it is to find participants, how many hours it will take, or how big the problem is. Instead, talk about:

"Leadership is the art of getting someone else to do something you want done because he wants to do it."

President Dwight D. Eisenhower

- Benefits – How will this project help *them*?
- Satisfaction – Why is the project worthwhile?
- Camaraderie – Who else is on the team?

"In addition," according to Carrington, "treat all of your team members with high regard. Value their time, their commitment, and their effort for your project. Don't *expect* them to accept the job. Appreciate them for their willingness to join in."

Rather than saying, "We need you to do more work," he approaches people with what they will get in return. For instance, "This will make your work easier. You'll get the data that you need faster. It could be a lot of fun."

Carrington has no control over the employees' paychecks. He can't fire them. So how does he get them to "volunteer?" He doesn't win them with coercion, but with sincerity. People aren't looking for more work and ways to give away their time. But they are looking for camaraderie, satisfaction and ways to make their own jobs easier.

What inspires people to act? Statistics don't. Facts don't. Feelings inspire people to act. People recoil when they feel that you are trying to take something away from them, like their time. Instead, look for what you can give. This way, people will participate willingly.

How to Win Support from an Adversary

Imagine this: You want a magazine to publish an article about your product. However, the editor of the magazine has never heard of your product, doesn't know you, and will not return your calls.

When Mark Davis was a marketing manager in London, he found himself in this situation. His client was a new author and Mark was trying to place an article about the author's new book in a particular periodical. He was certain the editor would be interested. She wasn't. She saw it differently. Because the magazine editor was strapped for time, had never heard of the author and didn't know Mark, she wouldn't gamble on it.

Mark was competing with thousands of other new books. Many authors were vying for the editor's attention. Still, despite the odds, Mark knew he had a good product and if he could just speak to her, he was sure the editor would agree. After numerous calls to her office had gone unanswered, he asked one of the magazine's columnists for guidance.

The columnist said, "That editor rarely receives thanks for her work. Readers seldom write letters to the editor when they are satisfied, but she hears frequently about mistakes." Based on this information, Mark prefaced his request to the editor with, "Thank you for putting out such a high caliber magazine."

The editor warmed to him immediately and took his call. Mark began by discussing what he genuinely appreciated about the editor's work. He then told her about his client's new book. She grew interested and agreed to run a story.

Was flattery the secret? I don't think so. Manipulation is transparent and weak. I think Mark's success came because he told the truth. He does admire the magazine. That's why he wanted to feature his client's book in that particular publication. If Mark had been lying to the editor, or insincere, I don't think he would have gotten the time of day from her.

How to Win Support from a Tyrant

What do you do when you report to a big, bad boss? When nothing you do or say is okay? When the tension between you is so thick and hard it could crack? When your boss doesn't want to see your face and it feels like you are walking on egg shells? How do you please a tyrant?

Joe, a friend of mine, went to work at a prestigious research institute. The work was what he had always wanted to do. He had an excellent staff. The offices were elegantly furnished. In many ways, the job was ideal, except his boss was difficult. She was notorious for going into rages during meetings and being hostile to those who worked under her. Most everyone lived in fear of her. No one wanted to be on the receiving end when she went on a rampage. Employees quit right and left. Those that stayed did lots of bad-mouthing the boss behind her back.

Joe, however, tried a different approach. He shielded those who reported to him, placing himself in between them and her line of fire. When he went into meetings with her, he adopted an attitude of patience and waited until her wrath passed. He didn't buy into her anger nor did he allow himself to fear her rage. He made a practice of noticing the good things this woman did and supported her when he could.

"I just wouldn't let myself approach her from a fearful point of view," Joe said. "I consciously pointed out her success. She was the director of a research institute that did excellent work. I focused on that, not her personality. I always gave her respect."

The result? "She left me alone," he says, "I was able to safeguard my team from her. She was very careful not to direct her animosity toward us."

Joe worked there ten years. He survived by not getting sucked into a high-pressure situation. He stepped back and avoided getting dragged into someone else's anger. Also, Joe did not allow himself to be a victim. He turned a bad situation to his advantage. In spite of the boss's temperament, it was fascinating work. While many employees left because they put their attention on her fury, Joe was able to stay because he expressed gratitude for her good qualities.

"If you treat people right, they will treat you right – ninety percent of the time."

President Franklin D. Roosevelt

Joe and his boss did not become best friends. She left him alone, which may be the best that can be expected in a situation like that. He also made a smart psychological decision to let his administrator get the satisfaction of believing that she was a world class employer.

If there are people like Joe's boss in your life, try this: appreciate them. Look for anything of value in difficult people and in tough situations. I've seen enormously uncomfortable predicaments resolve themselves by expressing gratitude.

How to Win Support from Yourself

Bradley Horowitz, VP Product at Google has this advice for young people: "Evaluate any opportunities through balance and detachment. Even though opportunities look glamorous, they may not be what they appear. Often things that look harder are better prospects. When you remove the veneer of pursuing a shiny opportunity, how does it make you feel? Set aside the expectations of those around you and check in with yourself. How do you feel about the job, the people, and the opportunity to grow? There are many ways to measure success."

Silicon Valley's legendary "coach" Bill Campbell was the mentor to Bradley's mentor. Campbell served on the board of directors of Apple and Intuit. He was known for the sage advice he gave to Apple's Steve Jobs, Google's Larry Page, and Amazon's Jeff Bezos, among many. Bradley says, "My meetings with him were not a deep dive into strategy. They were all around connecting, listening, appreciating people. We once spent an hour talking about being a step dad and how to navigate it. In many ways, he taught apple pie and football, but he commanded the attention of the people who built Silicon Valley."

"I've learned that people will forget what you said, people will forget what you did, but people will never forget how you made them feel."

Maya Angelou

Bradley Horowitz concludes, "So much of leadership is not about charts and strategies. It's about caring for people. Creating an environment where people can thrive. This takes a long time to learn. New managers are into doership. It is easy in a corporate setting to forget basic human needs. But to truly succeed, you must bring your whole self to work."

The only way to change the world is to deal with each day's concerns as they come. For instance, have you ever been fired from your job? Lost a major account? Been in love and then been dumped? When any circumstance robs us of our happiness, the actual feeling is similar. Dismal events look foreboding. People appear evil.

How do you respond at times like these? Do you succumb to malaise? Do you try to prove that you are right and others are wrong? Do you let your situation wear you down? Or do you give support to yourself as you would for a friend?

Late one night in Hong Kong, my coworker Sandra tapped on my hotel room door. We were scheduled to leave early the next morning for Osaka. Sandra's boyfriend had been with us, but while we were in China, he decided to break off their relationship and would return to the United States alone. They were about to have a farewell conversation and she was hurt and heartbroken.

Sandra held a responsible position in marketing. People were counting on her to hold it together. If she fell apart emotionally, our project was cooked. Still, Sandra was clearly upset and wanted to vent her frustration. Basically, she wanted to tell him everything he had done wrong throughout the length of their relationship.

When Sandra asked me for advice, I remembered being in a similar situation when someone posed a question that changed

"Whatever you are, be a good one."

Abraham Lincoln

my painful experience into a better one. So, I asked the question to Sandra, *"What would you want to express if you were going to die tomorrow? If this were the last chance ever to speak to this man, what would you say?"*

Suddenly, this irate young woman softened. Even though she was distraught about him leaving, she was grateful for what they had shared. They had enjoyed some wonderful times together. He had been considerate to her – mostly. She didn't think her anger could change him and, actually, she didn't want to change him. She just wanted to be appreciated.

So did he, it turned out. On the plane the next day she told me that they had a very pleasant parting.

The ending of a relationship can hurt, but Sandra used the opportunity to create a situation that she wouldn't regret in the future. Life is fleeting. She expressed her appreciation rather than her wrath and the relationship ended on a sweet note. Not long after that, Sandra met the man that she would marry.

Mark, Joe, and Sandra all wanted support – Mark from the editor, Joe from his boss, and Sandra from her boyfriend. All three made a shift from getting to giving. Instead of trying to *get* the editor to publish the story, Mark *gave* her a compliment. Instead of trying to *get* his boss to admire him, Joe *gave* his respect. Instead of trying to *get* even, Sandra *gave* her kind words and shared some enjoyable memories.

All three distinguished themselves by not succumbing to unfavorable circumstances. They didn't have to prove they were right. They didn't have to trick people into assisting them. They didn't have to use powers of persuasion. All they did was offer their gratitude. They gave gratitude and they received support.

"Nature does nothing in vain."

Aristotle

Yoga Wisdom
Breathing, Sacrifice & Surrender

Pullitzer Prize winning author Edith Wharton said, "The air of ideas is the only air worth breathing." I say, "Tell that to a drowning person." When you take your last breath, you're dead.

Scientists talk about the "rule of threes." Human beings, on average, can survive three weeks without food, three days without water, but only three minutes without air. Breathing exercises are an important part of yoga because fresh air is essential for life. We know its necessity, yet we hold our breath when we fear something, when we are confused and even when we are deep in concentration.

Breathing can help you to escape some sticky leadership situations. When you find yourself in any of these challenging circumstances, before you act – stop and breathe:

- Your fears are aroused.
- You feel incited to anger.
- You are enduring something that got out of control.
- Major conflicts.
- Injured pride.
- When you know what needs to be done but you waver.
- When you feel the need to defend yourself.
- You feel jeopardized.
- You've been dealt an injustice.

Breathe. When a mother is giving birth, she isn't told to "think about it." She is usually advised to "breathe through it." When you don't breathe, the body stiffens. Breathing relaxes the body and it becomes more flexible, more supple. Flexibility is an essential quality for a leader. Sometimes you have to be tough. Sometimes more collaborative. Knowing which is best in each situation is the skill.

Deep breathing helps you remain calm during unfavorable circumstances. You don't want to be caught flat-footed but you don't want to jump into action the moment an issue arises, either. As the world speeds up around you, taking a deep breath will give you the patience to handle pressure.

In a river, oxygen keeps the water fresh. In your lungs, as long as air is moving in and out, you don't die. An aerated body of water doesn't stagnate as it spills unhesitatingly over every cliff. No matter how far a river has to go, it presses on. When the water stops moving (as in a pond) there is decay. Along its journey, a river is joined by rain drops, melting snow, and spring waters. By letting other waters join in, a river will keep flowing. When it reaches its destination, it doesn't keep the water for itself. It generously pours everything into the sea.

What can we learn from the river? Resilience. Keep moving. Persevere, because when you stop, you stagnate. Allow others to join in, offering new ideas and fresh perspectives. Heart to heart exchanges with others renews the spirit. When you succeed, don't keep the credit. Give it away.

Barrie Risman from Montreal, Canada is the Co-Director of the World Spine Care Yoga Project. She describes yoga as a "metaphor for life, especially the quality of resilience." Barrie says, "Yoga gives you resilience, so you can appreciate the best within you, and accept those parts that you wish to change. This way, you expand your horizons."

Sacrifice. To understand sacrifice, study nature. The entire earth revolves on the principle of sacrifice. Everything that is created comes from the sacrifice of something else. The seed sacrifices itself to the soil; the day sacrifices itself to the night; the wood sacrifices itself to the fire. The word sacrifice means "to make sacred." People often define sacrifice as having to give something up, but it is more noble than that. When something is given up, a space opens for something new to be created. Parents sacrifice for their children even when their efforts go unappreciated. They give up a lot, but a human being evolves. Parents sacrifice themselves, then offer their sacred work to the world in the form of a child, the next generation.

Joe's story is an example of sacrifice on the part of a leader. He had the "right" to view his boss as an egotist. It would have been easy to make his boss "wrong." Instead, Joe sacrificed being right and saved a job that he loved and protected the people who worked with him, saving their positions, too.

Sacrifice is an important concept in yoga. Can we perform our work, our service to the world, as selflessly as nature and the elements perform their work for us? Compare the sacrifice of the river which gives and gives, to a pond which keeps its water for itself. The miserly, stingy pond eventually stagnates and dries up, while the river freely pours its water into the sea. There, heat from the sun causes it to condense. The moisture turns into clouds and then it falls again as rain, replenishing the river. It is a cycle that has gone on and on forever.

A mundane example of sacrifice is the gasoline in a car. It has to burn – it has to be sacrificed – for the car to move. If we try to preserve our tank of gas, we will never get anywhere. As a leader, if you are willing to make a sacrifice, you become a conduit providing nourishment needed by others.

Surrender. When a raindrop surrenders to the river, it becomes the river. It becomes greater, not less. In yoga, surrender doesn't mean giving up. Instead, you let go and go with the flow. And then, almost as magic, a great sense of relief and wellbeing comes over you. You feel satisfied. That's the glorious experience of surrender.

Picture this: You are on the phone waiting for tech support. It takes forever. You have a deadline, or at least a plan for today. Suddenly that plan is interrupted. Thwarted, you are exasperated. Finally, you realize that this is going to take a long, long time. When you let go and relax, you have surrendered.

One of my favorite stories of sacrifice and surrender is from the Jewish book of law, the Talmud:

A king and his son loved each other but they could not get along. Eventually, the son left home and went far away. After a while, word came back that the son was not doing well. The king sent a message to the prince, "Come home." But the prince was too proud. He sent a message back to his father, "I cannot." Then the king sent another message saying, "Just turn around and come as far as you can. I will meet you wherever you are." In leadership, you don't surrender your ideals. You only surrender your way of implementing them.

Gratitude. A human being's greatest support is gratitude. Appreciate where you are and who you are with. Whatever your situation, be grateful. Gratitude helps you stay on course to reach the horizon. Just as water is inexhaustible if kept fresh, gratitude is limitless in its ability to help you create energy and ideas. It is constantly invigorating. Gratitude (like breathing) is pure potentiality. The next time you are feeling sluggish, or stagnant, or things aren't moving – stop and breathe and practice gratitude.

"All things come to the person who is modest and kind in a high position."

I Ching

Pranayama. Yogis consider the breath to be an essential part of yoga, which is why they place so much importance on the breathing exercises called "pranayama." In Sanskrit, the first half of that word, prana, means life force. You want prana – life force – in every cell of your body because it gives you energy and keeps you healthy. The second half of the word, ayama, means to extend or draw out. Yogis believe they can extend life by slowing down the breath.

In contrast to deep breathing, pranayama is subtle and ancient and takes practice, preferably with an experienced instructor. Traditional pranayama exercises purify the blood and the respiratory system sending fresh oxygen to the brain, lungs and heart. Pranayama reduces stress, increases alertness, and boosts the immune system. It is a de-stressor because it relaxes the sympathetic nervous system which controls the release of stress hormones like cortisol. A regular practice of pranayama has been found to reduce apprehension and depression.

Are you someone who thinks you cannot meditate? Pranayama exercises could help you to focus and provide some of the same benefits as meditation. In your leadership role, pranayama could help you:

- Recharge your "batteries" and give you energy.
- Avoid reacting hastily or jumping into a conflict.
- Resist doing the easy thing just to get out of a sticky, uncomfortable situation and hold onto your principles while you wait until the right thing to do becomes clear.

The mind, the body, and the breath are intimately connected. Pranayama is a breathing exercise that reduces anxiety and despair. It increases energy, and decreases feelings of stress and overwhelm. Stressful thoughts cause your sympathetic nervous system, your fight or flight response, to burst into action.

You stop thinking and start doing, which is useful when you need it, but harmful when you don't.

Pranayama can reverse the symptoms of stress almost instantly by activating the parasympathetic nervous system through the vagus nerve which slows down your heart rate and calms both your mind and body. I suggest that you research the various pranayama techniques because each one has a specific effect. Some give energy. Some relax you. Meanwhile, learn one: alternate nostril breathing which is something you can do at work and it will immediately help you feel calmer.

Alternate nostril breathing: Never force the breath! This is not weightlifting. The breath is tender and subtle and extremely sensitive. Treat it with care.

For centuries yogis have used alternate nostril breathing as a practice to balance the right and left hemispheres of the brain. The practice is simple, yet quite powerful. The right nostril supports the sympathetic nervous system and heating functions in the body. Breathing through the right nostril is energizing. The left nostril supports the parasympathetic nervous system and cooling functions which calm you down.

Every few hours, all day and all night, the body switches between the right and left nostrils. At the moment the breath transfers from one side to the other, both nostrils open evenly. For a brief time, there is balance between the sympathetic and parasympathetic systems.

Do you feel peaceful watching a sunset? At sunset and sunrise, the body naturally balances the breath. For this reason, yogis have traditionally used dawn and dusk as the ideal time of day to meditate. You can create a "sunset-like experience" sitting at your own desk. Even 10 minutes a day of alternate nostril breathing can have a profound effect on your nervous system.

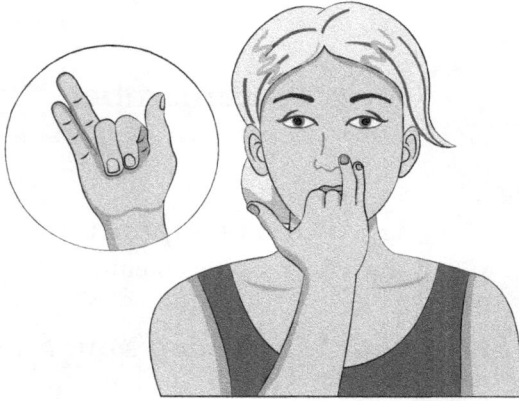

Alternate Nostril Breathing

- Sit quietly.
- With your right thumb, close the right nostril.
- Breathe in slowly through the left nostril.
- With your right ring finger, close the left nostril.
- Remove your thumb and breathe out slowly through the right nostril.
- Breathe in slowly through the right nostril.
- With your right thumb, close the right nostril.
- Remove the ring finger and breathe out slowly through the left nostril.
- Repeat until you feel calm. (It usually takes about five cycles.).

Gems to Remember

Gratitude is Support
John Frieda and his mentors

Serve Your Clients *and* Your Staff
Bonnie Callens needing more time

To Lead is to Appreciate
Recruiting people for **extra projects**

Appreciating Challenging People
Mark, Joe, and Sandra

Pranayama
Alternate Nostril Breathing until you feel calm

Exercise for Success

1. What is a human being's greatest support? Who and what has supported you in your life and career?
2. Who are your mentors? What have you learned from them?
3. What does this mean to you: "Love is not only for your growth, but also for your pruning," by Kahlil Gibran. How can you apply it to your professional career?
4. "To Lead is to Appreciate" – How will you implement this *Leadership with a Twist of Yoga* Principle?
5. What did you learn from "How to Teach a Task"?
6. How will you turn reluctant employees into willing participants?
7. List a few methods you can use to turn adversaries into people who support you.

"There is nothing in a caterpillar that tells you it is going to be a butterfly."

R. Buckminster Fuller

The Transformation of Ebenezer Scrooge and You

In this book, we've covered three of the *Leadership with a Twist of Yoga* principles:

- To Lead is to Connect
- To Lead is to Listen
- To Lead is to Appreciate

We've also explored the yogic wisdom found in stability, flexibility, balance, unity, dharma, detachment, breathing, sacrifice, and surrender.

Use these principles to care for and nourish your staff. Use them to honor and tend to yourself. They'll help you to see the greatness in people. They'll support you in overcoming obstacles and make you more creative in your role as a leader.

Managers who are willing to change themselves are the first to transform others. Changing ourselves and the teams that work with us are extremely grave matters. It is not easy and not everyone can do it. Those who can, must be free of selfish aims and must attempt it only when the time is ripe – at a time when they are enjoying the confidence of their people.

Ebenezer Scrooge changed his ways. In the closing paragraphs of "A Christmas Carol," Scrooge transforms. He doesn't suddenly become the world's greatest boss. Still, the old skinflint becomes generous – which makes him joyous and more pleasing to others.

As Dickens put it, "Many people laughed to see the change in him, but he let them laugh for he was wise enough to know that nothing ever happened on this globe for good at which some people did not have their fill of laughter. His own heart laughed and that was quite enough for him…May that be truly said of all of us."

With this hopeful outlook, *Leadership with a Twist of Yoga* comes to a close.

Thank you,   Shar McBee

About the Author

S har McBee, at age 26, had never received leadership training when she was suddenly put in charge of managing 500 people on a project in California. It was hard. Then a wise mentor taught her a secret that made it easy to get people to say YES.

A broadcast journalist, Shar left her job at CBS News and spent 10 years doing volunteer work all over the world. Working with (and supervising) thousands of diverse people from different cultures, she learned that people are not very different. Shar says, "A mother in a hut in India told me how proud she was of her daughter who could carry two pots of water on her head all the way from the village well. A princess in a moated castle in Belgium told me almost the same story. Different circumstances, of course, but with the same delighted and proud emotion."

Shar has been practicing yoga for 40 years. She's been writing and speaking about leadership for 20 years. Today she puts the two together in her keynote speeches and in this book, *Leadership with a Twist of Yoga.*

Other books by Shar McBee:
- To Lead is to Serve
- Joy of Leadership
- Leadership for Women

Contact: www.JoyofLeadership.com